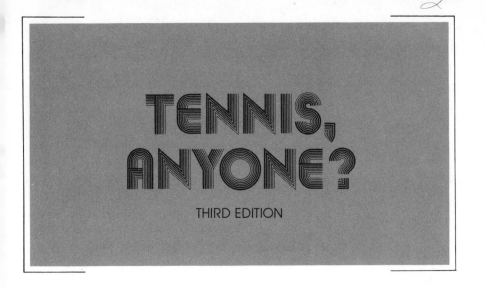

TENNIS, ANYONE?

THIRD EDITION

Dick Gould

Tennis Coach, Stanford University

 Mayfield Publishing Company

Library of Congress Catalog Card Number: 78-51946
International Standard Book Number: 0-87484-438-X

Manufactured in the United States of America
Mayfield Publishing Company
285 Hamilton Avenue, Palo Alto, California 94301

This book was set in Avant Garde Book and Helvetica Bold by
Chapman's Phototypesetting and was printed and bound by
R. R. Donnelley & Sons. Sponsoring editor was C. Lansing Hays,
Carole Norton supervised editing, and Susan Welling was
manuscript editor. Michelle Hogan supervised production, the
book was designed by Nancy Sears, and Bill Nagel designed
the cover. Cartoons by Jim M'Guinness and photos by
Dick Keeble.

CONTENTS

**The More
Advanced Player**
Page 35

**Background
of Tennis**
Page 75

PREFACE

What a thrill . . . the feel of a well-hit ball on the face of the racket, the exhilaration of running down a seemingly unreturnable shot, the satisfaction of diligent preparation leading to positive results, physical skill and conditioning, tactics and mental exercise, competition, friendships. . . . These are traits of one of the world's greatest and fastest growing sports — Tennis.

Yet tennis is one of the most difficult of sports to learn to play well. There are so many variables. The ball moves at different speeds, with different spins, and to different parts of the court. You must move after it, and then return it to a specifically defined area. Conditions such as weather and court surface may dictate strategy changes. You must not only play the ball, you must play another person.

Tennis can be complex, and so anything that can simplify and facilitate the learning of tennis is doing a favor to the sport. Perhaps this is why **Tennis, Anyone?** in its previous editions has been so successful. In the most simple and attractive way possible those editions provided a breakdown on how the ball should be hit and how to think on the tennis court.

Yet I have always felt there was room for improvement in the earlier versions. In this new edition, I have tried to keep the same basic simplicity that has made **Tennis, Anyone?** so popular, but at the same time have tried to make it more functional.

This almost completely new manual of photographs, diagrams, and step-by-step procedures is for the learner, the beginner as well as the advanced player. The progressions are clearly defined and easy to follow. The methods used are not just theory; for years I have used them in my large physical education classes and in my small private groups. In addition, my partner, Tom Chivington, and I train instructors to teach in our community recreation programs using these same methods. The large section for the advanced player, which has been completely rewritten, illustrates the same approach to stroke production and tactics that I use in coaching my advanced team players at Stanford. The approach to learning tennis outlined in this edition really works. A teacher can use this book as his or her "Bible" while each member of the class uses it as an individual guide.

I am excited with this new, usable book. I hope you will be also, and I hope that whether you are a novice or an advanced player this book will help you to enjoy a great game to the fullest.

ACKNOWLEDGMENT

Any "methods" publication represents experiences and ideas borrowed from a wide variety of sources which are adapted and synthesized to form one's own philosophy. However, I am especially indebted to my long-time friend Tom Chivington of Foothill College, Los Altos Hills, California. Together we have formulated most of the techniques and progressions presented in this book.

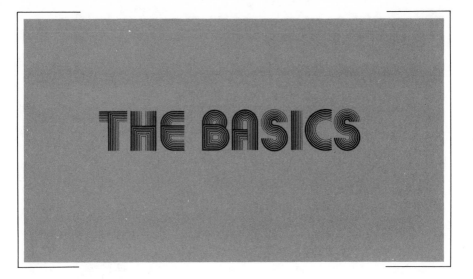

THE BASICS

In tennis several general concepts are significant.

Relaxation is the first. To help you relax while concentrating on what you are doing, try to slow down all your motions. Thus, in learning to hit a tennis ball, try not to hit hard. Instead, try to develop a feel of the ball on the hitting face of the racket; try to hold the ball on the racket as long as possible with a firm wrist, by hitting in "slow motion." Avoid jerkiness and abrupt motion. Develop a hitting rhythm by smoothing the swing out as much as possible.

Simplicity is a second important concept. The stroke should be mechanically as simple as possible, but with no sacrifice of control or power. Limit the variables. The more unnecessary movements you make during a stroke the greater the possibility that one of them will adversely affect the shot. Most motions in tennis are natural motions — the difficult thing for the learner is to let them be natural.

Repetition is another concept. This book constantly emphasizes doing one thing over and over again correctly so that you form a habit pattern. First you should know what you did incorrectly, but then — and just as important — immediately correct your mistake. As far as the basic strokes of tennis are concerned this makes the finish of each shot extremely important. By holding your finish for a second or two, you can observe much of what happened during the hit itself. Then, by correcting to the proper finish position, you can mechanically form a habit of doing it right.

Preparation is also very important. The majority of balls are missed because the inexperienced player does not get his racket back soon enough or does not move into position to hit as quickly and efficiently as he could.

Actually, we will be just as concerned with the start of the stroke as with the finish. We will break down the stroke so that you won't have to think about ball contact until you have prepared for the stroke.

Then, after ball contact, we will hold our finish to analyze and correct our feet, which allow us to have good balance, which in turn permits us to have the proper racket position. The premise is that your chance for hitting the ball well is enhanced if the start and finish are right, because what happens in the middle of the swing will then be right as well.

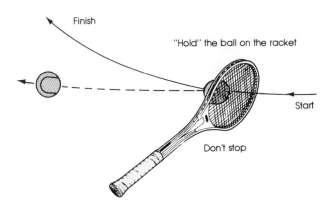

Finish

"Hold" the ball on the racket

Start

Don't stop

PRACTICING THE FOREHAND AND BACKHAND

The best way for you to practice as a beginner is with a partner who will toss the ball to you, the hitter. A backboard or wall at this point is not good because the ball rebounds so quickly that you do not have time to think what you did. It is not necessary to go to a tennis court to practice. A sidewalk, patio, or other paved area is all that you need.

Your tossing partner should stand about 25 feet from you. A chalk mark or circle target should be made on the paved area about 10 feet in front of you. If you use a tennis court, you may start on the service line, with your tossing partner just on the other side of the net.

Your partner should toss the ball underhand softly to the target when you, the hitter, are ready. Try to hit the ball back softly and with control so that the tosser can catch it at head level (which means the ball will clear the net by about 3 feet).

Tosser and hitter as partners using a "T"

The set position

The forehand grip

The Set Position and Forehand Grip

If you are on a court, face your partner who is on the other side of the net. Stand at the juncture of two lines, which we will call a "T," with your feet about shoulder-width apart, your weight evenly distributed on the balls of your feet, and your knees slightly bent.

With your right hand, grip the handle in a "shaking hands" position. (The palm of your hand should be almost vertical to the ground.) The "V" formed by the juncture of your thumb and index finger is thus squarely on top of the racket handle. Your thumb is completely around the racket handle and your fingers are slightly apart. You are now in the Set Position.

Start with a Forehand Grip on the racket. To get this grip, hold the throat of the racket lightly in your left hand so that the racket face is vertical to the ground as if it were "standing on edge." (The left-handed player should simply reverse hands in following these steps.) The racket is at waist level, pointing to the net. If there were an imaginary camera in the heel of the racket it would be taking a picture of your belt buckle.

Common Faults

1. *The positioning of the "V" is too far to either side of the top of the handle.*
2. *The grip is a hammer grip —the fingers are too close together.*
3. *The grip is too limp.*
4. *In the Set Position, the knees are too stiff or the body is bent over excessively from the waist.*

Hitting the Basic Forehand

Move a few inches to the left of the "T." From the Set Position facing your partner, "turn," and take your racket straight back by stepping with your right foot to the "T." This pivot puts you in a position ready to hit. The racket is still at waist level, with the racket head no higher than your wrist and with the imaginary camera in the heel of the racket now taking a picture of where you want the ball to go.

The ready position

Common Faults

1. *The initial step is back from the ball rather than to the "T".*
2. *The backswing is started too late. (The player runs several steps before starting the backswing.)*
3. *The player fails to turn completely sideways.*
4. *The wrist drags the racket back.*
5. *The elbow gets too far away from the body, preventing the racket from "standing on edge" and leading to excessive wrist movement.*
6. *The backswing is too high (too much wasted motion).*
7. *The racket head is above the wrist and the wrist is above the waist.*
8. *The arm is too straight and stiff.*

Ball contact

Once your racket is back in this Ready Position (not before) your partner will toss you the ball. Transfer your weight to the shot by stepping toward your partner with your left foot at about the time the ball bounces. Contact the ball well in front of your body with your wrist firm. Try to "carry" or "hold" the ball on the racket face as long as possible, and return the ball so softly that your partner can catch it.

Common Faults

1. *Poor footwork has prevented a weight transfer into the direction of the shot.*
2. *The ball is contacted too late or too close to the body. (This tends to make the racket head drop, and the swing "scoop.")*
3. *The wrist fails to remain firm (rolls over or "slaps" at the ball).*
4. *The swing from the Ready Position is down rather than up to the ball.*
5. *The knee is stiff and the body bent over.*
6. *The body opens toward the net too soon.*
7. *The ball is "hit at" rather than smoothly lifted, which results in too hard a hit — one the partner cannot catch.*

The finish

Always "hold" your Finish (see photo) until you have corrected in order your:

1. Feet

   a. All your weight is on your front (left) foot, which is flat on the ground and at a 45 degree angle to the net.

   b. Your back foot (right) has only the very tip of the toe lightly touching the court, and the back leg has relaxed into a comfortable stance.

   c. Now an imaginary line can be drawn touching both toes which goes toward where the ball is to be hit (use the alley line as a guide).

2. Balance

   a. Your front (left) knee is comfortably bent, but you are standing tall and erect from the waist with your shoulders level to the court.

   b. The racket swing has pulled your rear hip and shoulder around so that you are now squarely facing your partner.

3. Racket position

   a. Your wrist is at eye level and is firm so that the racket face is "standing on its edge" and so that the imaginary camera in the heel of the racket can take a picture of your left side. Thus the "tip" end of the racket head is pointing toward the top of the fence across the net.

   b. The racket is about 45 degrees beyond where you want the ball to go, which means that you will finish looking over your elbow toward your partner.

Common Faults

1. *Swing: a) The racket face fails to follow through far enough into the line of the shot.*

   b) The tip of the racket head either comes through too soon, or does not get around the outside of the ball.

2. *Feet: a) The front (left) heel rises off the court or the front foot turns open too much.*

   b) The weight is transferred sideways–the step is not toward the net.

   c) The back (right) foot has not come up to the very tip of the toe so the sole of the foot is not facing the rear fence.

3. *Balance: a) The legs are too stiff (the back foot slides up if necessary to allow the back leg to be relaxed), causing the body to bend forward from the waist.*

   b) The shoulders are not level, and the hips are not facing the net.

4. *Racket position: a) The wrist is not at eye level on the finish.*

   b) The tip of the racket head fails to point into the direction of the hit, and the racket has turned over.

   c) The swing is such that the elbow does not finish in front of the chin.

The backhand grip

Hitting the Basic Backhand

The backhand is very similar to the forehand in terms of technique and learning progressions. One of the main differences is how the racket is held.

Move a few inches to the right of the "T" from the Set Position. Facing your partner, change to the Backhand Grip by using your left hand on the throat of the racket to guide it back from the Set Position (so that the camera in the heel of the racket can take a photo of your right hip). Simultaneously, with your right hand make nearly a quarter turn so the palm of your hand is essentially on the top of the racket. The bottom of the top knuckle of your index finger rests

The set position

squarely on top of the handle. Your fingers are slightly spread and the thumb may give added support by being diagonally up the back of the handle.

Common Faults

1. The positioning of the top knuckle of the index finger is incorrect.
2. The grip is a hammer grip—the fingers are too close together.
3. The grip is too limp.
4. The grip has not turned enough from the forehand grip.

The ready position

"Turn" by stepping with the left foot to the "T." Take your racket back the rest of the way, with your left hand still lightly holding the racket at the throat. The backhand Ready Position is like the forehand in that your racket is at waist level with the racket head no higher than the wrist, and the camera in the heel of the racket now taking a picture of where you want the ball to go. However, your hitting arm is comfortably straight and your left hand is still lightly on the racket throat.

Common Faults

1. The initial step is back from the ball rather than to the "T."
2. The backswing is started too late. (The player runs several steps before starting his backswing.)
3. The player's side fails to turn completely or turns too late.
4. The backswing is too high (too much wasted motion) and the elbow is bent rather than comfortably straight.
5. The left hand lets go of the racket too soon.
6. The racket head is above the wrist and the wrist is above the waist.

Ball contact

Once you have taken your racket back to the correct Ready Position, not before, your partner will toss you the ball. Transfer your weight at about the time the ball bounces by stepping toward your partner with your right foot. Contact the ball with your wrist firm and well in front of your body. Hit the ball back softly by lifting it out so that your partner can catch it.

Common Faults

1. *Poor footwork has prevented a weight transfer into the direction of the shot.*
2. *The ball is contacted too late or too close to the body. (This tends to make the elbow bend, the racket head drop, and the swing "scoop.")*
3. *The left arm fails to help initiate the forward swing by guiding the racket toward the ball.*
4. *The wrist fails to remain firm, causing the racket head to drop.*
5. *The elbow bends and thus leads the racket to the ball and causes the swing to be down.*
6. *The body opens up too much toward the net.*
7. *The ball is "hit at" rather than smoothly lifted, which results in too hard a hit–one the partner cannot catch.*

The finish

Always "hold" your finish (see photo) until you have corrected in order your:

1. Feet

   a. All your weight is on your front (right) foot, which is flat on the ground and at about a 45 degree angle to the service line.

   b. Your back foot (left) has only the very tip of the toe lightly touching the court, and the back leg has relaxed into a comfortable stance.

   c. Now an imaginary line can be drawn touching both toes which goes toward where the ball is to be hit (use the alley line as a guide).

2. Balance

   a. Your front (right) knee is comfortably bent, but you are standing tall and erect from the waist with your shoulders level to the court.

b. The racket swing has pulled your rear hip and shoulder around so that you are now facing at a 45 degree angle to where you want the ball to go (not quite as much of a turn as on the forehand).

3. Racket position

a. Your wrist is at eye level and is firm, so that the racket face is in the same plane as your shoulders and the imaginary camera in the heel of the racket can take a picture of your front (right) foot. In other words, the racket head, due to the nature of the backhand grip, is higher above the wrist than on the forehand.

b. The racket arm has moved about 45 degrees beyond where you want the ball to go. The left hand has lightly followed the racket at the start of the swing, so that it now rests just in front of the belt buckle.

Common Faults

1. *Swing: a) The racket face fails to follow through far enough into the line of the shot.*

   b) The tip of the racket head either comes through too soon (wrist slap) or does not get around the outside of the ball (elbow bend).

   c) The left hand lets go of the racket too soon.

2. *Feet: a) The front heel rises off the court or the front foot turns open too much.*

   b) The weight is transferred sideways. The step is not toward the net.

   c) The back foot has not come up to the very tip of the toe.

3. *Balance: a) The legs are too stiff, which causes the body to bend forward from the waist.*

   b) The shoulders are not level and the body is facing too much toward the net.

4. *Racket position: a) The wrist is not at eye level.*

   b) The racket tip fails to point out into the direction of the shot and finish above the wrist.

   c) The finish is not far enough around the ball to the right of the body.

HINTS

1. As it is difficult to have the correct racket position without good balance, and as it is almost impossible to have good balance without good footwork, always **check and correct** first your feet, then your balance, then your racket position.

2. "Holding" in tennis is important, for it allows you to see what you have done during the swing. By "correcting" what was wrong, a **habit** for doing the right thing can be formed. Ask your partner to help you with your corrections. Never hit the next shot until you have corrected the first.

3. Although you will feel restricted and stiff at first, try to develop a soft, slow, fluid hitting motion. Think of a gradual "slow motion" swing — of "catching" the ball, and of "holding" it on the racket, rather than of hitting "at" the ball.

4. You have undoubtedly found that even with a target for the tosser, the ball is not always where you want it, which makes transferring your weight directly into the shot difficult. Try taking some Adjust steps as the ball leaves your partner's hand before you commit yourself to your final step into the shot. Thus if the ball is too close, you can adjust back quickly. If it is too far away, you can adjust forward quickly so that you can still step into the hit.

5. To help you with your learning (or if someone else is helping you), "think" — or say — the following words as you do your stroke: "Turn," meaning to pivot and take the racket back to the Ready Position; "Toss," meaning the moment when your partner throws the ball; "Adjust," meaning to take a couple of quick steps that position your feet so you will be able to transfer your weight into the shot; "Step and hit"; "Hold," meaning to "freeze" at the end of the shot in order to see what you did; "Correct," meaning to progress from the "hold" position to correct your feet, balance, and racket position in order to make the correct swing a habit.

6. As you get a feel for what you are doing and start to develop the rhythm of the swing, have your partner toss as you start to take your racket

The running backhand

back rather than waiting until it is all the way back in the Ready Position.

7. To help you develop accuracy and control, see how many of 10 forehands you can hit in such a way that you can correct your finish and your partner can catch the ball. (Your partner should need only one ball if you can consistently hit it so it can be caught.) Apply this test to the backhand as well.

Common Faults

A ball-throwing machine, if you have access to one, can be a great device for "grooving" your strokes. So that you will not be rushed and can think about what you are doing: take the racket back before the ball is released; use a fairly slow ball speed and a slow time interval between shots; "adjust" your feet when the ball is in the air; "hold" and "correct" each finish. (To practice your accuracy, put a target on the opposite side of the net, such as a ball can or a towel to aim at).

Hitting Running Forehands and Backhands

Wide Balls   You are beginning to feel comfortable returning balls without having to run a great distance for them (what we call stationary forehands and backhands). You are gaining more control of the ball and you have little need to correct your finish, since the basic swing has become a habit. Now you are ready to begin hitting forehands and backhands for which you must run a greater distance. Begin by taking a couple of recovery side-skips away from the "T" (to the left for a forehand, to the right for a backhand). Now "turn," by stepping with the foot nearer the direction you wish to go and at the same time take the racket back to Ready Position. Run smoothly to the "T." Your partner will toss after you reach the "T" provided you are waiting on the correct foot (right for the forehand and left for the backhand) and provided your racket is in the proper Ready Position. "Adjust" your feet to the toss as the ball leaves your partner's hand before stepping into the shot. Hit and "hold" your finish to **check** and **correct** your feet, balance, and racket position. "Recover" by side-skipping back to your original starting point.

Moving back for a deep forehand

HINTS

1. When you feel comfortable with this, and when you are "holding" and correcting well, ask your partner to toss the ball as you near the "T" so that you never have to come to a complete stop before stepping into the hit. (It is important, however, to realize that you, the hitter, **always** initiate the action. If the tosser tosses before you have turned and started to run, you will have to play "catch-up" with the ball, and will probably not be able to transfer your weight correctly into the line of the shot.)

2. You will soon be able to get the feeling of constantly moving. In other words, as soon as you have recovered, push off, turn, and go right into your next hit. **Always** pause at the finish, however, and then make any corrections necessary. In this manner, many balls can be hit in succession within a short time.

3. If you use a ball machine, turn and take the racket back and begin running to the spot the ball will most likely be **before** the ball is released. (This gives you, the inexperienced player, time to reach the ball without being hurried.) "Adjust" your feet while the ball is in the air, and "hold" and "correct" the finish before recovery skipping back to the starting point. Use a fairly slow ball and slow timing interval between shots when you first start out. Try to develop a rhythm on shots and make all of them smooth. (If the machine oscillates so that you can alternate forehands and backhands: run to the ball, hit, hold, and then skip back to the center of the court. When you get to the center, immediately turn and run for the next ball.)

Deep and Short Balls   To hit the basic forehand and backhand, usually you run to either side for balls. However, you will soon find that you must not only move back for a high, deep ball but up for a short, low ball. To practice this, begin with the "T" as your home base. Your partner will now toss one ball high and a couple of feet beyond the circle, and the next ball short and a couple of feet in front of the circle.

For the **deep ball** step back (right foot for the forehand, left foot for the backhand) as you turn. The object is to run far enough back to allow the ball time to descend from the peak of its bounce to your waist level before you hit it. Since you are returning the ball further back in the playing court, you must return the ball higher so that it will float deep — thus, you will be hitting a ball that approximates a lob, a ball hit quite high above the net.

Take your racket back to a lower Ready Position than normal. Do this by leaning slightly backwards, which lowers the rear shoulder (right shoulder for the forehand, left for the backhand). This puts the racket head slightly below your wrist and therefore permits you to hit up to the ball. Your partner should toss high as you start back. This gives you time to adjust your feet and still be able to step into the line of the shot. Lift the ball up so that it goes to your partner with a reasonable arc — it should "fall down" to your partner. "Hold" your finish and "correct" any faults.

Now start moving forward for a **short ball** by taking the racket halfway back to the Ready Position and stepping forward (with the right foot for a forehand and the left foot for a backhand). As you approach the "T," your partner tosses short and you turn the rest of the way. Adjust your feet and step into the shot. (Since the short ball is usually also a low ball, lower the racket head in the Ready Position slightly below the wrist, as you did on the deep ball.) Hit by lifting the ball up to your partner, and "hold" and "correct" the finish. Repeat the cycle by hitting a deep ball next.

HINTS

Both the deep and short balls must be returned by using a higher trajectory than normal — the deep ball in order to carry it deep, the short ball in order to clear the net. Think of contacting the bottom of the ball by starting the swing not only with the racket head lower than usual and below the wrist (and in turn, the ball), but by beveling the racket face slightly open (perpendicular to the anticipated flight of the hit ball).

By returning only one ball at a time you have as long as you need to correct each shot. However, as you form habit patterns and gain confidence in correctly hitting and con-

Moving up for a short backhand

trolling tossed balls, you are ready to move into a more realistic situation in which you will return balls that are hit to you. This is a most important stage of your stroke development for, if you are careless, and overanxious to return the ball, all that you have practiced with tossed balls will be forgotten.

Thus we will break the practice rally down into three learning progressions — starting the rally (one-hit rally), returning the ball (two-hit rally), and keeping the ball in play (Forever Rally).

Start up close — about 50 feet from your partner (if you are on a court, you should be on the opposite side of the net from your partner and just beyond a service line "T"). Standing up close rather than "full court" helps you to remember to hit softly, and gives you time to "correct" your finish before the ball can be returned.

The practice rally position

The one-hit rally and catch

THE PRACTICE RALLY

Since most balls hit by beginners are forehands, we will emphasize the forehand rally. If you are on a tennis court, use the alley as your target. Stand outside the alley so that if the ball lands in the alley it will be to your forehand. Or, use the serve court but stand off center so that most balls landing in the serve square will be to your forehand. This will allow you to prepare early and without being hurried, by being able to take the racket back to the Ready Position before your partner hits the first ball. As a hitter, your objective is to have the hit ball approximate a tossed ball. The ball should be hit in a soft arc as opposed to a beeline shot, so as to make it go up and then "fall down" into the alley well short of an imaginary extension of the service line.

Starting the Rally (One-Hit Rally)

Turn and take your racket back to the Ready Position. When the racket is completely back, toss the ball up so that it bounces in front of you toward the net. When the ball leaves your hand, quickly take a couple of "adjust" steps to ensure that you can transfer your weight into the line of the shot. Hit the ball up softly into your partner's target area and "hold" and correct your feet, balance, and racket position. Your partner can gain valuable practice in judging the ball by taking his racket back when you do, adjusting his feet quickly to your hit, and then positioning himself so as to be able to step into the hit ball and catch it with his free (left) hand. If the ball comes to him high, he learns to adjust back and let the ball drop down. If the ball comes low, he learns to bend his knees in order to catch it at waist level. If the ball is to either side, he gets practice by adjusting either away from or toward the ball. "Play catch" with your partner in this manner until you can control the speed and trajectory of the ball and yet always "hold" and "correct" the finish.

HINTS

1. To help you hit softly in an arc (a) lower your racket head slightly below your wrist in the Ready Position by lowering your back (right) shoulder; (b) start with your hitting arm slightly bent at the elbow and held so that the imaginary camera in the heel of the racket takes a picture of where you want the ball to clear the net; (c) toss the ball up, so that it bounces high and allows you to hit it from underneath; (d) step forward and let the front (left) knee bend, but stand up straight from the waist; (e) follow through completely, but slowly.

2. To help you control the direction of the hit, try to feel the ball on the racket face as long as possible with a firm wrist — "push" the ball into the direction of the hit and don't be in a hurry to follow through.

3. As a goal, see how many out of 10 balls you can hit softly within the target area and with a good finish.

Returning the Ball (Two-Hit Rally)

Both you and your partner "turn" and take your rackets back to the Ready Position at the same time as in the one-hit rally. Hit the ball softly to your partner, who will return it if it lands in the target area. "Hold" your finishes and "correct," especially to see if you have "adjusted" your feet to allow yourself to step into the flight of the ball. (Let the ball go by if it comes back to you.) Practice until you and your partner can complete at least 10 successful two-hit rallies.

Keeping the Ball in Play (Forever Rally)

It should be an almost natural progression from the two-hit rally to "keeping the rally going." As long as you are not hurried and the ball lands in the target area, return the ball to your partner.

The cross-court rally

HINTS

1. Emphasize having your racket back **before** the ball lands on your side of the net, but "hold" your finish ("correct" if necessary) until your shot lands on the other side.

2. Since you are hitting almost all forehands, there is no need to come back to the Set Position after each shot. If, however, the ball does go to your backhand and you have the time, return it with the backhand.

3. See how many hits in succession you can do.

4. Try a cross-court rally. Instead of using the alley and hitting straight ahead, use the diagonally opposite service square as your target area, and hit across the court. Emphasize turning to the Ready Position so that your side and shoulders are diagonal to the cross-court service square. Toss the ball so that you can step diagonally to the cross-court target area rather than straight toward the net.

5. Gradually move back to full court, hitting softly and with some arc.

6. Repeat the above process using mostly backhands, except for the first hit which will be a forehand. (Stand so the backhand is exposed to the target area.)

7. Use the backboard. After you have had some practice with the Forever Rally, a backboard may be used to advantage. The same principles apply — don't hit too hard, practice just forehands; then, just backhands (without returning to the Set Position). Hit to a target, such as a chalk mark on the wall.

The Set Position for the serve

The backswing and ball toss:
Both arms down

Both arms up

The "L" position

PRACTICING THE SERVE

You should begin to practice the serve at least by the time you have started the one-hit rally. In many ways it is simpler than the forehand or backhand because the ball is not moving fast at you or away from you; instead it is controlled by you. Practice is also easier, for you can do it yourself without a partner. If you are not near a court, you may draw a circle on a wall about 4 feet from the ground, stand about 40 feet away, and hit to the target.

Most people who find the serve difficult to learn are those who fail to think of the serve in progressive steps. For example, it is hard to throw the ball up correctly if you are already worrying about dropping the racket behind your back. It is hard to drop the racket if you are thinking ahead to the contact itself. Thus the serve presentation is divided into two parts — the serve toss and backswing, and the forward swing (the hit itself).

The Serve Toss and Backswing

Start in the Set Position, with your left side toward the net. The weight is on your back (right) foot, with both hands on the racket and the racket pointing to where you want the ball to go. Use a forehand grip on the racket. (See photo.)

Let both arms drop together toward the front (left) leg. Now concentrate on the toss. Transfer your weight onto your left foot as your left arm begins to extend up for the toss and as your racket starts to travel past your toes in a wide arc toward the fence behind you. As your left arm reaches up, release the ball. Toss the ball about 2 feet above your extended left hand and about 6 inches in front of your left toe.

Begin to bend the racket arm at the elbow, without using any wrist motion, as the elbow reaches shoulder level. It continues to bend to about 90 degrees so that the racket is up just above the head. "Hold," letting the ball fall back into the tossing arm, and check to see if: (1) your weight is on your left foot; (2) your left arm is fully extended upward (it follows through even after the ball has left your hand), and (3) your racket arm is high, with the elbow at shoulder level, and bent so that the racket tip points up above your head.

The forward swing:
Racket drop

Common Faults

1. *The ball toss and backswing are not coordinated (the left hand lowers to a position beside the front leg rather than in front of it, thus preventing the arms from rising together).*
2. *The ball toss is too low (the left arm does not follow through high enough on the toss).*
3. *The ball toss is too far back. (Either the weight doesn't transfer forward on the toes, or the left hand flicks the ball instead of "placing" it in the air.)*
4. *The arc of the backswing is cramped (the racket wrist turns over on the backswing, causing the elbow to bend before it reaches shoulder level).*
5. *The backswing is not in the hitting plane. In other words, the tip of the racket head fails to point to the fence behind the hitter.*
6. *The backswing and ball toss are hurried (because the server is prematurely concerned with ball contact).*
7. *The hitting elbow is not at shoulder level and the tossing arm is not fully extended up at the conclusion of the backswing.*

Contact

The Forward Swing

Now, upon catching the toss and getting your racket arm into the correct position ready to hit, begin the forward motion by letting your racket arm continue to bend at the elbow so that your racket falls behind your back. As the racket drops, bring your racket arm forward in a throwing motion, extending it high above your left foot. (Your tossing arm drops across the body as your racket arm rises up.) Snap your wrist up and forward to the imaginary ball, follow through, out, and then down to your left side, letting your back (right) heel rise off the ground. Make this entire throwing motion as smooth as possible. Keep repeating this motion in two parts — the backswing and ball toss, and then the forward swing.

Finish

Common Faults

1. The racket does not drop far enough behind the back (or, the racket is dropped by "breaking" the wrist rather than by bending the arm at the elbow).
2. The right side of the body turns forward too soon before ball contact.
3. The hitting motion is down to the ball rather than up. Not enough wrist action is used.
4. The hit is too hard and doesn't have enough arc. (This means the body is not relaxed and the swing not loose enough, so that the body "muscles" the serve.)
5. The body falls off balance (because the left foot does not stay anchored flat on the ground).

HINTS

1. Think of the serve progressively — first the toss, then the hit; especially if you are having trouble with the toss. Do this by practicing the serve in three parts:

a) From the Set Position, let both arms drop to the left leg. Now transfer the weight forward as your left arm tosses the ball into the air. Catch the ball in the hand of the completely extended left arm. "Hold," to check that the weight is on the front foot and the left arm is pointing straight into the air.

b) After practicing Step (a) several times, try adding the full backswing. Begin in the same manner by letting both arms drop from the Set Position to the left leg. Now, as your weight begins to transfer, let both arms separate — the left arm proceeding up with the toss while the right arm continues to travel past the toes toward the fence behind you, finally bending into its "L" position. "Hold," to check three things; that the weight is on the front foot, the left arm has caught the ball while remaining fully extended upward, and the right arm is in the "L" position with the elbow at shoulder level and bent 90 degrees so that the racket is above your head.

c) After completing a couple of ball tosses including the backswing, and after you have caught the ball and made your three checks (weight, tossing arm, racket arm), then complete your forward swing by letting the racket drop behind your back as it moves forward to the ball. Hold your finish to check that your right foot is up on the tip of the toes and that your racket has finished across your body to your left side. You should be completely balanced, facing the net.

2. Now stay as relaxed as you can. Work on smoothness, not power. Try a few full easy swings without the ball toss. Try to hit softly up on the ball. (Actually hit it in an arc. This will help you to drop the racket behind your back.) Toss the ball a little higher than necessary to give you more time to drop the racket behind your back. If you still have trouble dropping the racket, think of trying to make your wrist touch your shoulder before you swing up to the ball.

3. Balance after you hit. Keep your front (left) foot flat on the ground to give you a solid base of support, but let the back leg relax and the foot turn up onto the toe. (Keeping the right foot back forces you to hit only good tosses, for the foot can not step out to reach a bad toss. It also helps to give you the proper rhythm of the racket drop and shoulder turning action up into the hit.)

JIM McGUINNESS

BASIC NET PLAY

Now, with a knowledge of the basic strokes, you are ready to begin net play. You will need a partner, but you do not need a tennis court for practice. We will talk first about the forehand and backhand volleys, and then about the overhead. For the volleys, you and your partner should stand about 10 feet from each other (on opposite sides of the net if you are on a court). Start net play in the Set Position with your racket head at chest level and your arms slightly forward. The volley is divided into two parts: the preparation, and the hit.

Practicing the Forehand Volley

To prepare for the forehand volley, step forward with the right foot as you push the palm of your racket hand forward (let go of the racket with the other hand). Turn your body slightly so that you are facing the racket squarely. (The racket face is now approximately parallel to the net, with the racket head slightly above the wrist and well in front of your chest. You should be bent slightly forward from the waist so that your head is near the racket. Your hitting elbow is well in front of your body.)

When you have prepared by "showing" the hitting face of your racket to your partner, he softly tosses underhand to the racket face. For the hit, step toward the ball on to the left foot and "block" the ball back to your partner's head, keeping your wrist firm. "Hold," so that the racket face is still toward the net after the hit. (In other words, if another ball were now tossed, it also would rebound back to your partner.)

The forehand volley:
Prepare

Contact

Finish

The backhand volley:
Prepare

Contact

Finish

Practicing the Backhand Volley

Prepare by pushing your right hand forward as you change the grip. (This puts the racket basically parallel to the net so that the racket face is now in a position to hit the ball.) At the same time, shift your weight onto your left foot and turn slightly to face the racket squarely. You should bend slightly forward from the waist so that your head is close to the racket.

Now your partner tosses to the racket and you step on to the right foot toward the ball. Keep the left hand still, but with the right arm push the racket forward to hit, or "block," the ball with a firm wrist back toward your partner's head.

Common Faults

1. *Too much backswing is used (this causes the ball to be contacted late and not in front of the body).*
2. *The wrist fails to remain firm on contact (this causes the racket head to drop below the wrist on the finish).*
3. *The player volleys "from the waist" rather than "from the chest."*
4. *The ball fails to be punched from the elbow on the forehand, or fails to be pushed from the shoulder on the backhand.*

HINTS

1. "Hold" the finish and check to see that your racket face is parallel to the net and the racket head is still above the wrist; your weight is all on your front foot with the toe of the back foot lightly touching the ground.

2. Always do the volley in two parts: prepare, and hit. Your partner tosses only after the preparation has been completed.

3. The forehand volley is basically hit with elbow action; the backhand volley is more from the shoulder. In both cases, the racket stops abruptly on contact.

4. Always keep your elbows well in front of your body. (Don't start with the elbows against your side.)

The overhead:
Ready position

Contact

Finish

5. The volley can also be practiced against a wall. Stand 4 or 5 feet from the wall and volley the ball **up** against the wall. Hit softly and hit just forehands or backhands — not both. Don't return to the Set Position. This is a good way to practice your footwork and to get the idea of keeping your hitting elbow and racket in front of your body.

Practicing the Overhead

For the overhead, your tossing partner should be about 10 feet from you, but should stand off to the side so that the hit ball does **not** go back to him. The ball should be tossed underhand high and almost straight up, which gives you time to "adjust" your feet to the ball. The overhead is also practiced in two parts — the preparation, and the hit. To **prepare** you take a step back with the right foot (turning your left side toward the net). Pick your racket straight up from the Set Position to a position similar to the serve Ready Position. (Your hitting elbow is at shoulder level and your arm is bent so that the racket is above your head.)

When you are in the Ready Position the ball is tossed. "Adjust" your feet by sliding forward if the ball is short, or by sliding back if the ball is deep. For the hit itself, transfer your weight on to your front foot and let the racket drop only a little behind your back (to your shoulder blade) as the hitting shoulder turns forward. Bring your racket forward and up to contact the ball, using a firm snap of the wrist. Keep the follow-through short almost as if "tapping" the ball. "Hold" to see if your weight is balanced on your front foot with your back toe turned, and your wrist "broken," with the racket head tip pointed in the direction of the hit.

Common Faults

1. The player fails to move under the ball (most overheads are missed because of bad footwork).
2. The player overswings, instead of relying enough on the wrist action.
3. The eyes fail to watch the ball closely enough (usually because the ball drops too low and makes the head drop).

HINTS

1. Use your left hand to "point" up to the ball as it is in the air. This will help you to keep the ball in front of your body.

2. As you gain more confidence, you can gradually begin taking a bigger swing by letting the racket drop more behind the back and by following through more with your arm.

3. If you don't have a partner, it is still possible to practice against a wall. Hit the ball down to the ground so that it bounces up to hit the wall. It will continue to go up after glancing the wall and will come back toward you. Keep the "rally" going by hitting the overhead down to the ground again.

ORGANIZING YOUR PRACTICE

Most of us need some direction on how to spend our practice time. It is easy to get bogged down with one particular stroke and neglect developing other important shots. Thus, here is an example of six structured practice sessions for beginners, and six sessions for players with some slight experience. Each practice session will take about an hour to complete and includes a **review** of the items covered on the previous lesson, as well as orderly introduction of a **new skill**. While it would be nice to have a court on which to complete the sessions, this is not essential. A driveway or almost any paved area will do. You need only a couple of balls and a willing partner. (For serving, it helps to have a wall or fence to serve against.) You might have a court yourself, or even be in a small class that has 6 people on a court, or a larger class that has 12 to 18 people on a court. It usually doesn't matter how many are in the class. The object, remember, is to make yourself your own teacher.

An Outline of Practice Sessions

Six One-Hour Practice Sessions for the Complete Beginner

Practice Session I
1. Forehand swings (stationary)
2. Ball toss
3. Ball toss and hit to partner — forehand (stationary)
4. Backhand swings (stationary)
5. Ball toss and hit to partner — backhand (stationary)

Practice Session II
1. Forehand swings (running)
2. Ball toss
3. Ball toss and hit to partner — forehand (running)
4. Backhand swings (running)
5. Ball toss and hit to partner — backhand (running)

Practice Session III
1. Forehand swings (running)
2. Ball toss and hit to partner — forehand (running)
3. Backhand swings (running)
4. Ball toss and hit to partner — backhand (running)
5. Serve toss and backswing
6. Full serve swings

Practice Session IV
1. Serve toss and backswing
2. Full serve swings
3. Serve
4. Forehand swings (running)
5. Ball toss and hit to partner — forehand (running)
6. Backhand swings (running)
7. Ball toss and hit to partner — backhand (running)
8. One-hit alley rally (to partner)
9. Two-hit alley rally

Practice Sessions V and VI
1. Serve toss and backswing
2. Full serve swings
3. Serve
4. Forehand swings (running)
5. Ball toss and hit to partner — forehand (running)
6. Backhand swings (running)
7. Ball toss and hit to partner — backhand (running)
8. Two-hit alley rally
9. Forever alley rally

JIM MCGUINNESS

Six One-Hour Practice Sessions for the More Advanced Beginner

Practice Sessions I and II
1. Forehand swings (running)
2. Ball toss
3. Ball toss and hit to partner — forehand (running)
4. Backhand swings (running)
5. Ball toss and hit to partner — backhand (running)
6. One-hit alley rally (to partner)

Practice Session II:
Add two-hit and forever rallies

Practice Session III
1. Forehand swings (running)
2. Ball toss and hit to partner — forehand (running)
3. Backhand swings (running)
4. Ball toss and hit to partner — backhand (running)
5. Two-hit alley rally
6. Forever rally
7. Serve toss and backswing
8. Full serve swings
9. Serve

Practice Session IV
1. Serve toss and backswing
2. Full serve swings
3. Serve
4. Forehand swings (running)
5. Ball toss and hit to partner — forehand (running)
6. Backhand swings (running)
7. Ball toss and hit to partner — backhand (running)
8. Two-hit alley rally
9. Forever rally
10. Forehand volley
11. Backhand volley

Practice Session V
1. Serve toss and backswing
2. Full serve swings
3. Serve
4. Forehand volley
5. Backhand volley
6. Forehand swings (running)
7. Ball toss and hit — forehand (running)
8. Backhand swings (running)
9. Ball toss and hit — backhand (running)
10. Cross-court rally — two-hit and Forever (gradually move back from serve court to full court)
11. Overhead

Practice Session VI
1. Serve toss and backswing
2. Full serve swings
3. Serve
4. Forehand volley
5. Backhand volley
6. Forehand swings (running)
7. Ball toss and hit — forehand (running)
8. Backhand swings (running)
9. Ball toss and hit — backhand (running)
10. Cross-court rally — two-hit and forever (gradually move back from serve court to full court)
11. Overhead

USING THE BASIC STROKES
IN A GAME SITUATION

It is natural to progress from the cross-court rally introduced in the preceding section and the last two advanced beginner practice sessions into a discussion of basic doubles strategy.

Tennis is most fun when all competitors are of nearly equal ability. If you are in a class, a quick way to find other players of like ability is to have a series of "drop out" rallies. Simply rally with another player using the two service squares as your target. When one of you misses, he drops out. The player "winning" the rally receives a point, and a new challenger comes in to play the winner.

After about 15 minutes the players who have accumulated the most points on the various courts should congregate on one court; those players who have won the lowest number of rallies (who have the fewest points) should gather on another court; and those who are in-between should meet in equal-sized groups on the other courts. Repeat this rally process with the players in your new group one more time.

Now you should be in a group of players of roughly similar ability. In fact, when you and your partners are ranked vertically on a "ladder," competition takes on an added dimension because you can challenge individuals on the ladder, giving yourself a chance to move up or down in the ranking.

Introduction to Basic Doubles Grouping

Doubles is a game of **position**. Each partner is primarily responsible for his own side of the court and should be able to cover any return the opponents hit, if he knows where to be in a certain situation. We will begin by describing the basic starting position of each player. Then we will show how a player moves from his Home Base by adjusting his position to the most common situations that occur. We will discuss the positions and responsibilities of the net players first, and then of the backcourt players.

The Net Players

The emphasis in doubles at any level is to get to the net so you can hit down on the ball and also hit to a greater angle of the court in an effort to win your point. Since the server's

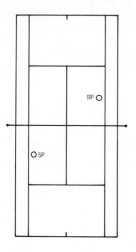

The net players' home base

S   Server
SP Server's partner
R   Receiver
RP Receiver's partner

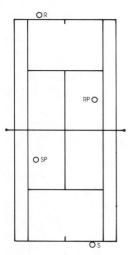

The backcourt players' home base

partner and receiver's partner are not engaged in the start of the point they can begin at the net.

The net player's Home Base position is approximately 10 feet from the net (halfway between the net and the service line) and 1 or 2 feet from the alley. The primary responsibility of the net player is to let no ball pass by him on the alley side of the court but, by his presence, to force all balls to the middle. In addition, the net player is constantly looking for the **poach** — that is, a ball that can be intercepted and cut off.

The first **rule** of doubles is, therefore: "The net player moves to the side of the court the ball is on." (He must watch the ball all the time, except when his partner serves.) The net player's movement consists of taking a side-skip or two in either direction from his Home Base with each ball that is hit. If the ball inadvertently goes to the opposing net player, he then covers the center of the court as well as possible.

The Backcourt Players

The server begins in the backcourt since he must stand behind the baseline to serve. The receiver is also near the baseline because he must let the serve bounce before he returns it. Basically, the server and the receiver take a Home Base position bisecting the middle of their respective sides of the court (or, more correctly, bisecting the angle the ball may be returned to).

The Cross-Court Rally

Doubles play starts with the cross-court rally, since the server directs the ball diagonally across the court to the receiver. The primary objective of the backcourt players, then, is to keep the ball going back and forth to each other and away from the net players. In addition, the backcourt players should try to keep the ball high enough over the net so that it lands deep in the opponent's court. The best way to do this is with a high, floating ball rather than with a "beeline" ball which barely skims the top of the net. After each shot, the backcourt player returns to his Home Base about 1 or 2 feet behind the baseline on the center of his side of the court.

If a return goes short, the backcourt player moves into midcourt to hit it but, rather than remaining in "no-man's-land" (the center of the playing court — where most balls bounce), he moves up and joins his partner as a net player. The **rule** is, "The backcourt player should join his partner at

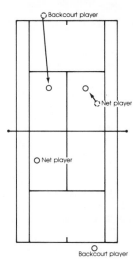

Home base positions when both partners are at net

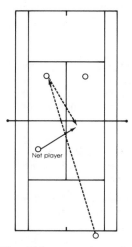

When both opponents are at net, the opposing net player looks for the poach if his partner returns low, down the middle

net any time he can get there and be set by the time his opponent hits the ball." This is the first example of when the backcourt player comes to net. (If he has had to move well inside the playing court to return the ball, he then has time to get the rest of the way to the net.)

Two Partners at the Net

When both partners are at the net, a new Home Base must be assumed. If they remain only 10 feet from the net, it is too easy for their opponents to hit the ball over their heads (a lob).

Thus, the **rule** is, "When a second player joins his partner at the net, both should assume a set position just inside the service line, about 15 feet from the net." Although they have now sacrificed some angle (since they are farther from the net), by moving forward from their new Home Base they can still be close enough to volley the ball (hit it before it bounces). Yet, by putting their rackets in the air and moving a couple of steps back, they can return any lobbed ball before it bounces by hitting an overhead.

When both opponents are at the net, the opposing net player is placed in a tenuous position. He stays at the net if his partner is able to return the ball low. When this happens he can most likely move to the center and poach, since his opponents will be volleying up. If, however, his partner lobs, he retreats toward the baseline, primarily so he won't get hurt by the opposing team's smash, but also to give him a little more time to react to the ball.

When both opponents are at the net, they should direct the majority of balls, whether lobs or drives, down the middle of the court to avoid giving their opponents any unneces-

sary angles of return. Each player is now totally responsible for his own side of the court. He should allow no ball to bounce — either in front of him or behind him. He should take all balls early and on the fly.

HINTS

Each team takes basic positions, with one partner at net and the other partner in the backcourt. Backcourt players begin a cross-court rally.

1. Backcourt players keep the ball away from the net players, and hit the ball high enough over the net to keep it deep. (You will soon see how the high, bouncing deep ball either sets up the poach for your partner or elicits a short return on which you can move into the net).

2. Net players slide with each shot to the side of court the ball is on, always watching the ball. Remember first to cover your respective alley but also to look for the poach.

3. After a backcourt rally of three or four hits, direct a ball to the net player to be certain the opposing net player covers the center of the court, and to be certain the volleying net player moves diagonally forward to the ball.

4. If the ball lands short, the backcourt player moves up to it and continues to the net to join his partner. Both partners assume the new Home Base position just inside the service line.

5. If any player gets out of position, stop the rally and analyze each player's position in terms of how the positioning rules apply.

The Lob in Doubles

The Short Lob   During the backcourt rally diagonally across the court, you probably experienced a short lob that inadvertently went to the opposite net player. This situation affects the position of each player in different ways.

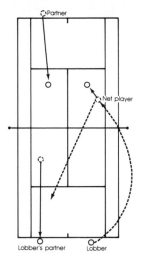

Positions when a short lob is hit

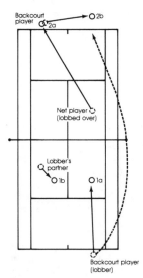

Positions when a deep lob is
hit over the net player's head

1. Lobber a) comes to net
to b) new net player's
home base
2. Player lobbed over a)
crosses and goes back,
while his partner b)
crosses and returns with
a lob

For the lobbing team, the **rule** is, "Any time a player can smash the ball down, the opposing net player retreats quickly toward the baseline." From the point of view of safety alone, this makes sense since the ball may very well be hit at the net player. Another **rule** is, "Any time an opponent contacts the ball no matter where you are on the court, stop and get set." This gives you a chance to react and change direction to go after the ball. Then, after the ball is hit, continue back to a position behind the baseline with your partner. (If the overhead is hit short, and you must move up to hit, both of you return up to the Home Base position at the net.)

For the player hitting the overhead the lobbed ball is in the air long enough to allow the partner to also come to the net. **Rule**: "Come to the net whenever you can be set in your new Home Base by the time your opponent contacts the ball." The partner hitting the overhead must remember to adjust back to his new Home Base after his smash so that he and his partner can cover, with equal effectiveness, either the volley or the overhead.

The player who is lobbed over, upon seeing that he cannot reach the shot with his overhead, immediately yells "switch" to his partner. He then crosses over to the other side of the court while diagonally moving back toward the baseline. His partner crosses over to the other side of the court to return the ball. (He must realize the lobbed ball will bounce high and thus he retreats well behind the baseline in order to let the ball drop down from the peak of its bounce to approximately his waist level.) He retrieves the ball with a high lob himself since he realizes that both his opponents are probably at the net, and he must therefore give his partner time to get back to the baseline.

Once both partners are side by side, either up at the net or back at the baseline, they stay side by side. If one goes back for an overhead, then the other also goes back. If one moves in for a short ball, the other moves in also.

The Deep Lob   If the lob gets over the net player's head, a new situation is presented. In this case the lobbing player can take advantage of what is basically a defensive shot by using the time the ball is in the air to get to the net. **Rule**: "Come to net whenever you can be set in your new Home Base by the time your opponent contacts the ball." The lobber's partner must remember to adjust back to his Home Base just inside the serve line, since the opponent's return will also probably be lobbed, and since his partner is now at the net with him.

HINTS

Start the point with the basic cross-court rally. After two or three returns, try lobbing over the opposing net player.

If the lob attempt is short:

a. The lobber's partner retreats toward the baseline, but gets set as the ball is smashed.

b. The smasher's partner joins him at the net at the new Home Base.

If the lob is deep and clears the net player's head:

a. The net player yells "switch" and crosses diagonally to the other side of the court toward the baseline.

b. The net player's partner covers, by crossing behind the baseline in an attempt to lob the ball high and deep.

c. The original player hitting the lob joins his partner in the new Home Base at the net.

Adding the Serve and Return

Now that you have the feel for the basic situations that most commonly occur in doubles (the backcourt rally with one partner up, the short ball, the short lob, and the deep lob), let's add the serve and serve return by talking more specifically about the positions in which the players start the point.

The server should generally stand in about the middle of his side of the court. The receiver should assume a Home Base that bisects the angle to which the server may hit. (Usually this is about 1 foot from the alley, but may vary somewhat depending on whether the server is serving from close to the center or wide, by the alley.) The receiver should start at the baseline but may move back if his opponent's serve is very hard, or move inside the baseline if his opponent's serve is very soft. (If he starts inside the baseline he should either move back after the return or, if the serve is very short, he may use the return as an approach shot and move up to the net with his partner.)

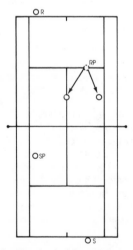

Positions to start the point

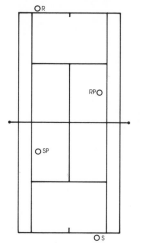

Positions after a good serve return

The server's partner should start in his normal Home Base at the net. The receiver's partner should begin on the middle of the service line on his side of the court. This is only a temporary position (if he were to start at the normal player's home base and his partner were to hit a bad return – in other words, a ball to the net player – there would be no way for him to cover the center of the court). If the return inadvertently goes to the opposing net player, he does his best to cover the center of the court. If the return is good – in other words, back to the server, he moves up to his normal Home Base and the point continues.

HINTS

1. Keep the rotation moving by having each player serve four points, or by playing a 9-point tie break (see the section on scoring).

2. If players get out of position, stop the point and analyze the positions in terms of the basic rules already presented. Then start over again.

3. If you are in a group of six people and are with an instructor, try rotating in two groups of three. The instructor can be a permanent fourth player, controlling the course of the point. Also, the six players can be divided into two different ability groups, to make the doubles points more realistic.

JIM McGUINNESS

THE MORE
ADVANCED
PLAYER

STROKES

There is no magic point in your tennis development at which you should begin to learn more refined strokes. It may be several years before you have mastered the forehand and backhand drive, the basic serve, and the net shots described in the first section. But the more you play the more you will develop idiosyncrasies. You will develop your own style, which may well differ from the rather regimented presentation already given in this book.

For example, you may have learned that you cannot hit a one-handed backhand well, and thus you begin to hit with two hands on the racket. You will develop more rhythm in your strokes, and will probably start taking the racket back to the Ready Position (the circular backswing) in a more fluid manner. You will find the spin plays a larger part in control as you begin to hit harder, and you will at times use more overspin. You will also begin to use underspin occasionally. You will realize the importance of ball spin on the serve. As you learn to hit harder you will naturally begin to place more emphasis on attack and you will realize that the basic strokes are only a means to an end. Much more important in determining your success will be how you use the strokes you have already developed in a playing situation. Before we get into a discussion of advanced singles and doubles tactics however, let us look closely at variations of the basic strokes. First we will talk about the backcourt player.

The Backcourt Player

The Two-Handed Backhand   If you are relatively small and lack strength in your wrists, or if you have a sore elbow, you have probably found that you can keep the racket head moving through the flight of the ball with less strain on your arm if you hit the backhand with two hands. (Most of the increasing number of top players using two-handed shots today began tennis at an early age and needed the extra hand to give support to the racket.)

Set position

Start of backswing

Ready position

There are some disadvantages to using two hands. For example, it puts a premium on precise footwork, it affords slightly less reach, it can cause confusion when you are learning to volley, and it reduces flexibility for spinning the ball, especially for an underspin on approach shots and return. But there are advantages too: precise stroke, heavy ball pace and penetration, a tremendous amount of disguise in passing shots, and extra help in getting the racket head quickly around the outside of the ball in difficult situations.

Most two-handed players hold the racket with two forehand grips, with the right hand at the base of the grip and the left hand higher up on the handle. Only one grip is used (the grip does not change from the forehand grip). Most two-handed players use a fairly straight backswing and always have a complete pivot since having both hands on the racket pulls the front shoulder well around toward the net.

The footwork is even more critical in two-handed shots than in one-handed shots. If you are late getting to the ball and have to step to the side (parallel to the baseline) to reach it, your back side (left side of the backhand) is prevented from getting into the shot; thus you are forced to rely too much on your wrists to get the racket head through the flight of the ball. Try to position yourself, therefore, to step into the line of the shot so that your rear hand can help pull your rear hip through on the Finish. On the hit itself, try to keep the racket face on the ball for as long as possible by letting the racket tip come around the outside of the ball on the Finish. To do this, keep the wrists firm, and on the Finish be certain that the racket head is not turned over, and that the

Contact

Finish

racket and arms are pointing in line into the direction of the shot. Think of the two-handed backhand as a left-handed forehand.

Common Faults and Hints

1. *The wrists tend to droop at the end of the backswing. Rather keep them firm and in line with the racket.*
2. *The racket tip fails to point into the line of the shot because the elbow points out or up. Thus, on the finish for the backhand keep the right elbow down and even, with the right arm bent a little as the left arm straightens out.)*
3. *The footwork has been slow and late.*

The circular backswing

The Circular Backswing   In the first section, we presented a straight backswing, which is simple to execute and, at the beginning level, is certainly adequate. As you gain more experience you will become less structured in your stroke production. As we talk about more overspin you will realize the racket cannot simply follow directly into and through the flight of the ball but must of necessity start a little lower and finish a little higher. A straight backswing can discourage this flexibility.

It is easy to learn a circular backswing. First begin in the Set Position, with your elbows bent so that the racket head is at chest level (as for a volley). When you turn, "think" the tip of the racket head back first (in other words, be careful not to let your wrist drag the racket back). Your arm should be relaxed at the elbow, although the elbow remains comfortably close to your body. The backswing is coordinated to take place with the turn and the pivot, and the arm is relaxed at the elbow to make the motion fluid and circular. At the conclusion of the backswing the racket head is up near the shoulder, since the arm is not yet straight and you can still run comfortably with the racket in this position.

As you transfer your weight into the hit, your arm tends to straighten, which allows the racket to drop into its hitting position below the ball. As the swing continues, the racket head comes forward and up to the contact point. It takes a little longer to drop the racket head in an uninterrupted motion below the ball and then bring it forward, but you will soon sense the basic rhythm and be able to adjust your

timing. The advantages are the inherent rhythm and racket-head speed that the racket drop gives to the swing. It also affords an easier adjustment to the lower ball. How far the racket drops depends simply on how low the ball is and how much topspin you wish to put onto the ball.

The Overspin or Topspin   As you hit harder you will need to get more spin on the ball to keep it in the court. The object is to make the ball drop or dip as it clears the net, especially against the net rusher. As you add more topspin you will realize that you tend to lose some depth and penetration — two items that are more important on hard-court or grass surfaces than they are on clay or slow indoor surfaces.

The basic principles are the same throughout the stroke. There are two variations, however. One is to start lower and finish higher. Your racket begins further below the ball at the end of the backswing, and finishes higher above the ball on the Finish. The forward swing is more steeply upward through the ball.

The other way to put more spin on the ball is to roll the wrist over the ball on contact. Most players who rely primarily on this technique to gain topspin on their forehands have turned their grip rather excessively from the classic Eastern forehand. (This is the one described in the section on basics in which the wrist is laid back slightly on contact, tending to limit wrist roll.)

By dropping your wrist on the backswing so that the racket points toward the ground and the racket face is partly closed, you can roll your wrist over the ball. The extreme example of this is the offensive or topspin lob. However the wrist roll is hard to control and is not encouraged for most players.

For more topspin, drop the racket more under the ball and finish higher with a steeper follow-through

The backhand slice

The Use of Underspin   So far we have talked only of overspin. The forehand is almost always hit with overspin. It is just as natural, however, to hit the backhand with underspin. It is common for top players to use underspin on most backhands when rallying from the backcourt. The underspin shot also affords control. Since the racket head starts forward from a position above the ball rather than dropping below the ball, it is a much shorter swing. A primary advantage, then, is easier timing, especially when taking the ball on the rise such as on an approach shot. In addition, the ball can be hit later in relation to the body, which is an advantage when you are hurried. The underspin ball may be hit with a great deal of pace and penetration, as on the "slice," or may be hit with extreme touch so that it tends to die on the court, as on a "drop shot." The primary disadvantage is that the ball does not curve or dip downward as fast as in the topspin. Thus the underspin is not nearly as effective as a passing shot against a net rusher.

For the **slice,** the racket passes down and through the flight of the ball at less than a 45-degree angle. The racket head is above the wrist and the anticipated point of contact at the Ready Position; the racket face is "beveled open." The forward swing is slightly down and forward through the line of the shot. The wrist stays firm. The follow-through is still with the wrist at eye level, but the racket face is beveled slightly open. Occasionally on the forehand side, especially when a player may "chop," the ball changes pace. The **chop** is best defined as being like the slice except that the forward swing passes down at more than a 45-degree angle — there is more dip in the forward swing itself.

The forehand chop

Another variation of the underspin shot is the **drop shot,** which softly clears the net and lands short in the court. Use it to pull your opponent to the net or even to produce an outright winner if he is too deep in the court. It can turn into a liability, however, if you use it too much or attempt it from too far back on the court, for if your opponent can get to the ball in time it will be an easy winner for him. To hit the drop shot, the racket starts well above the wrist and the backswing is very short. The forward hitting motion is down and under the ball. As the racket comes under the ball, open the racket face more so the ball is given a slight upward and forward lift, yet keep the wrist firm. The racket finishes at eye level with the face still beveled open.

The drop shot

The Server

The Spin Serve Grip   Good servers hit the majority of their serves with spin. Spin makes the ball loop and this increases its chance of going in. The first thing to do in learning the spin serve is to change the grip from the forehand to one approximating the backhand. This grip allows you to brush the ball more easily instead of meeting it "flat on." When first attempting to hit the serve with this grip you will probably find that your serves land short and to the left. Instead of getting bogged down with hitting detail, simply try to hit up and swing more to the right. This will tend to give you proper wrist hitting action for the most widely used spin serve — the topspin serve.

The spin serve grip

The Spin Serve Ball Toss   The spin serve is divided into two parts: the backswing (including the ball toss and the leg action), and the forward swing (including the different wrist actions for the different spins). During the ball toss, the body turns more sideways than it does for the basic flat serve. This causes the tossing arm to make a letter "J" motion. The tossing arm will be rising parallel to the base line and pointing less toward the opponent. As you toss the ball, bend both knees forward; this has the effect of causing your heels to rise up from the court. The racket is now up and poised in a "ready to hit" position.

The "J" ball toss and backswing

The Topspin Serve   Toss the ball a few inches in front of the base line, but slightly over your front shoulder (if it were to drop it would land in front of your heel, instead of in front of your toe). Allow the ball to fall a couple of inches from its peak. The racket, after it has dropped behind your back, can now hit up over the back of the ball (think of "brushing" up the back of the ball with the edge of your hand). The swing is then almost parallel to the baseline as the racket goes up to the ball. The back shoulder comes forward much later in the swing than it does in the basic flat serve. To help, be certain your left arm, as it drops, tucks across your chest while the racket moves up to the ball, and that your back toe does not rotate forward before ball contact.

As you contact the ball, "reverse" your wrist so that the tip of the racket goes forward over the top of the ball (see photo). (Concentrating on the racket tip ensures that the ball will have penetration and pace.) The legs are straightened upward as the racket goes up to meet the ball. You will now be a little off balance, so let the right leg fall across the baseline into the playing court on the finish. This, in turn, will result in the Finish being to the left of the body.

To help you learn the proper wrist action, practice this serve into the backhand side of the ad court. Also, it is important that your wrist not open up so that the palm or the hand faces the sky on the backswing. If this happens and the wrist "breaks" prematurely it will cause you to hit under and around the ball rather than up over the top of the ball.

The topspin serve forward swing

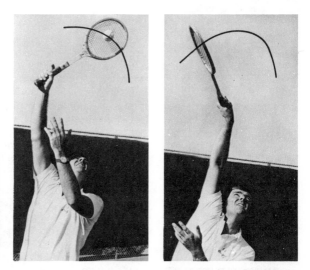

Wrist action and ball contact, the American twist serve

The American Twist This serve is an extreme version of the topspin serve. The ball is tossed even farther behind the body, causing the body to bend farther back to reach it and creating an extreme "hitting up and over" reverse wrist action on the ball. This increased hitting up on the ball tends to make it kick up higher after it bounces. And, since the ball is tossed farther behind you and therefore hit more on the inside, the wrist reverse makes it curve into the player as it approaches him and then kick away in the opposite direction after it bounces. (This serve can create a strain on your back and is not used much today, primarily because the excessive topspin tends to make it land short in the receiver's court.)

The Slice Serve This serve is important, for it allows the right-handed player to serve wide into the deuce court, and the left-handed player to serve wide into the ad court. It is distinctly different from the topspin serve in that the hit is around the outside of the ball rather than up the inside. The key element is that of surprise. While the easiest way to hit around the outside of the ball is to throw the ball to the right, this also makes it easier for your opponent to "read" what you are planning to do. Thus, try to hit around the outside of the ball by throwing it more forward. A common fault is to pull down on this serve. Make yourself keep your head and body up as long as possible during the hit. Also when practicing the serve don't be afraid to serve the ball too wide by using extra spin.

Hitting angle and ball contact for the slice serve

The drive serve return

The Receiver

The use of the serve return and court positioning will be discussed later. Here we will confine ourselves to a brief discussion of the mechanics of returning the serve and the resultant spins that may be used. The serve return motion is relatively short — somewhere between a high volley and a regular forehand or backhand. To help keep your backswing short, think of two things: first, a full pivot and getting the weight onto the foot nearest the ball, which gets the racket back; second, keeping the hitting elbow well away from your body (in front of it) during the pivot.

A straight backswing is used to take the racket back for most serve returns. The racket goes back at about chest level rather than at waist level, since the ball bounces higher than on a normal drive. This allows you to position your racket so you can still hit through the flight of a higher bouncing ball. Stay forward on your toes as you pivot, and lean a little forward with the front shoulder. This encourages you to transfer your weight forward into the shot as you hit.

The Drive Return   Meet the ball with the racket beveled flat. Lift the ball slightly up as your racket moves forward. To get more topspin, drop the racket below the ball on the backswing and finish higher above the flight of the ball on the finish.

The Underspin Return   For the underspin return, open the racket face on the backswing and hit flatter through the ball, keeping the racket face beveled open on the Finish. If you want to **chip** the ball low, use a softer swing to meet the ball as you put underspin on it.

The finish of the underspin return

> **Hint**
>
> In all cases, meet the ball in front of and well away from your body, as your weight moves forward.

The low forehand volley

The low backhand volley

The Net Player

The Approach Volley   As you learn to hit harder and play more aggressively, you will come to the net more often. In many cases, such as when coming to net behind your serve, you will have to hit a transition volley from midcourt before getting to your Home Base position. The important thing to remember is to always be "set" when your opponent contacts the ball so that you can change direction and react to the return. The simplest way to get set is simply to jump to a "split" stop, landing on the balls of both feet at the instant your opponent contacts the ball. "Read" the return, then while the ball is in the air react forward to it with a couple of quick steps, "set" again, and then step into the hit.

Usually this approach volley will be low, since it will be contacted from about where the ball would bounce. If the ball is low you may want to open your racket face slightly on contact to put a little underspin on the ball and give it depth. Keep your wrist firm, meet the ball well in front of your body, and lift the racket forward into the flight of the ball with a short but smooth follow-through. If the ball is high, you can move in more quickly after getting set. The racket may go back farther on the backswing since you may turn more. Remember, many high volleys from midcourt are hit into the net, therefore hit out on the ball rather than down. The ball that is waist level or higher can be hit very flat.

The Drop Volley   Once you are at the net you may find occasions where you want to drop the volley very softly over the net. This situation might occur when your opponent is deep in the playing court and his return is dipping low to you. For the drop volley, open the racket face on contact and relax your wrist. Use very little follow-through. This takes the speed off the ball and makes it land short. However, as in the drop shot from the backcourt, remember your opponent will probably win the point if he can actually get to the ball.

The drop volley

The Overhead   Overheads landing near the service line should be hit very flat. Get your feet set if you can. As the lob goes deeper, however, you may want to put some spin on the overhead to give it more control and, in essence, play it almost like an approach shot to help give you time to get back into position at the net for the put-away on the next shot. If the ball goes behind you, the most effective way to transfer your weight and hitting shoulder into the shot is to use a scissor kick in midair by thrusting the right foot forward as you hit.

The overhead smash (the scissor kick)

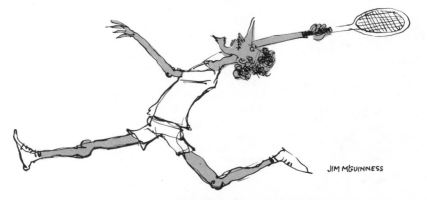

JIM McGUINNESS

SINGLES STRATEGY

The player with sound strokes is at a distinct advantage in a tennis match but it is essential to realize that strokes are only a means to an end. Strokes enable you to make the best use of strategy, and once you have learned them you must try to use them as intelligently and efficiently as possible.

In our discussion of strategy, we will talk about the initial shots of every point — the use of the serve and the use of the return. We will discuss defensive tennis — the importance of keeping the ball in play, and of keeping it deep. Next, we will cover when to hit cross court, down the line, and short. Then we will progress into offense — when and how to come to the net, off both ground strokes and serves. Finally, we will talk about what to do against the net rusher, both during the rally and on the serve return. An outline of our sequence is:

- The use of the serve
- The use of the serve return
- Keeping the ball in play
- Keeping the ball deep
- When to hit cross court
- When to hit down the line
- When to hit short
- Approaching the net on a ground stroke
- Approaching the net after a serve
- Defending against the net rusher during the rally, and on the serve return

The Use of the Serve

As a beginner, you were probably primarily concerned with just getting the ball into play and maybe to your opponent's backhand. As you gain more confidence you can use more variety on your serve (speed, spin, and placement) and start to use the serve to offensive advantage.

The Importance of the First Serve   Your philosophy as a server should be to try to get at least two-thirds of your first serves in the court. Don't waste your first serve just because you are entitled to another. You can serve more aggressively (and yet competitively) on your first serve because you have another chance but, remember, if you miss your first serve, it is like the pitcher falling behind the batter. There is much less opportunity to take the offensive. The receiver knows this and will play accordingly, especially since he can expect that the serve will go to his backhand.

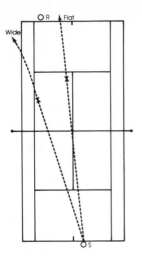

Serve wide to pull your opponent out of position

On important points, however, when it is important to keep the pressure on your opponent, a much higher percentage of first serves must be good, even if it means serving less aggressively. If you are substantially behind, you might as well serve more aggressively and try to get back in the game quickly. Above all, don't double fault. It is just like walking the batter. If it occurs at "ad out" it is just like walking in a run.

Mix Up Your Serves A hard, flat serve to the backhand may be your most effective serve but you cannot use it all the time, any more than a pitcher would use only a fast ball. Keep your opponent guessing and off balance.

Serve **wide** to your opponent if:

1. You have a natural angle, such as a slice to the forehand in the forehand court or a twist to the backhand in the backhand court.
2. Your opponent undercuts (slices) most returns. This may mean he cannot return well with the drive, the natural return for a wide ball, especially when hitting cross court.
3. Your opponent assumes a faulty set position—too far behind the baseline or too far to one side of the court.
4. Your opponent backs up to return a wide serve instead of stepping in and cutting off the angle.
5. Your opponent moves in close to return in an attempt to come directly to the net. A wide serve pulls him off the court and makes it more difficult for him to get to the net.
6. There is a concentration letdown (after a long point or a long game). This is a good time for a wide serve to the forehand.

Serve **tight** to your opponent (for example, to his forehand in the ad court) if:

1. He normally takes a big swing at his return—a ball close to his body makes a big swing difficult.
2. He is hurting you with angle returns. Don't give him the angle, especially on big points.

Serve **high** (top spins or twists) to your opponent if:
He cannot return a high ball well. Many players cannot hit well through a high ball.

Serve **deep** to your opponent if:
You want to significantly cut down the effectiveness of his return, especially on second serves where he may be moving in to get more angle. (If you are having trouble serving with depth, throw the ball forward more and hit with less spin.)

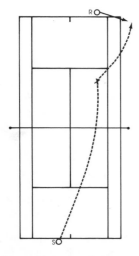

Serve wide to slow down an attacking receiver

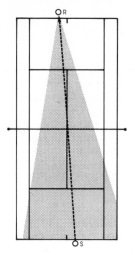

Serve down the middle to cut down angle on the return

Vary Your Pace   Some receivers rely on the pace of the serve for the effectiveness of their return. Don't hesitate to use more spin and slow the ball down occasionally, even on a first serve. When you serve a hard, flat serve, remember the net is lowest in the center and the ball gets to the receiver sooner down the middle than when it is hit wide. (The ball will be coming back quickly as well, but with little angle for the return.)

The Use of the Serve Return

A good server has the initial advantage, whether or not he comes to the net behind his serve. However, a good return can neutralize that advantage. **Positioning,** as was mentioned earlier, is important. Quickly try to find a Home Base for returning a particular player's serve.

If you have to move wide to hit the return, move diagonally forward to cut down the angle. Don't let a wide serve drive you back. Likewise, don't charge the ball. A common beginner's mistake is to run forward into the ball instead of turning. Stay down with the return—the front knee always gives some on the return. Don't rise up on contact.

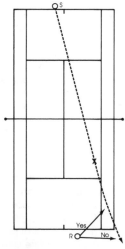

Don't let a wide serve drive you back

Even though the basic return is a rather flat drive, vary your returns. Stand back a little farther sometimes, take a bigger swing, and drive some returns with substantial topspin. Or, shorten your backswing and move into the returns (especially when your opponent has had difficulty serving and has been serving short), even to the point of going to net behind the return occasionally. Remember, the earlier you take the ball, the shorter the swing and the more underspin you'll put on the ball (which means, on serve returns, a slice or a chip).

Most of all, think positively. Look at returning a serve as a challenge, don't just stand in a batter's box and wait motionless for the pitch. Be on your toes; take a little jump up into the air just before the serve is hit to help you get ready. Make the server know you are there. Move around. Make him think of serving down the middle by standing wider in the court. Make him try to hit too good a second serve by standing in close. Make him change his serving rhythm by standing far back. Don't look up to return until you are really concentrating and mentally ready.

Determine before the ball is served where you will return it and what kind of a return you are going to use. Don't wait

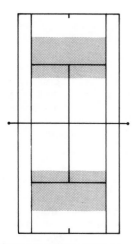

Don't get caught waiting for the ball in "no-man's-land"

to see what kind of serve it is and then react to it. **You** take charge; **you** have a plan — to hit soft cross court, or to hit hard down the line, etc. Generally keep the pressure on your opponent by getting a high percentage of returns in play. But don't be afraid to "go for it" by hitting harder or playing the returns closer to the line on occasion. You can gamble more when you are returning the serve than when you are serving. Don't wait for the server to lose the serve — make him lose the serve. You **win** the return game.

Keeping the Ball in Play

Assume Proper Court Position   You must know where to wait for your opponent's shot in order to best be able to return it. Each player should stand 1 or 2 feet behind his baseline, approximately in the center of the court. Be careful not to get caught in "no-man's-land" (midcourt) unless you are purposely going to the net. Balls will bounce behind you or at your feet if you are in the midcourt. These are difficult shots to return, and you will usually be forced to hit them up (defensively). If you have to run into no-man's-land for a short ball, return quickly to your Home Base behind the baseline or go on to the net. Don't remain in no-man's-land.

Bisect the Possible Angle of Return   Always return to a position behind the baseline that bisects the possible angle of your opponent's hit. For example, if the ball is being hit from Point A, assume a set position at Point B, slightly to the right of the center mark (see diagram).

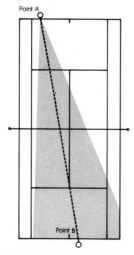

Bisect the possible angle of return

Play Percentage Tennis

Make Your Opponent Hit the Ball   This is the first and foremost rule in tennis for the advanced as well as the beginning player. Concentrate on keeping the ball going back to your opponent. Don't let him off the hook by trying an unnecessary shot, missing, or getting caught out of position. You need only hit the ball in the court one more time than your opponent to win the point. If you can keep the ball in play, you can pressure your opponent to hit a placement to beat you.

Try to Balance Errors and Placements   Unnecessary errors — balls that could have been returned — cause 75 percent of all points lost. Only 25 percent, on the other hand, are lost because of placements — shots hit so well they

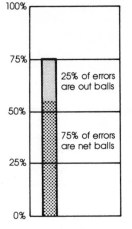

75% of points end in
unnecessary error

could not have been returned. Three-quarters of the unnecessary errors are because the ball hit the net, and only one-quarter because the ball landed out of bounds.

Inevitably, you will make errors. Even in championship tennis it is a rarity to have a perfect balance of errors and placements. But play percentage tennis and cut down on unnecessary errors. The player who wins is the one who makes fewer errors — and the one who makes fewer of them at critical times. Never try to hit the ball better than you have to to win the point; don't try a $10 shot if a 10¢ shot will accomplish the same result. This is why some people are better competitors than others.

Play Each Point   Point by point play puts tremendous pressure on your opponent. It is possible to lose more points ·than you win and still win the set. Know the critical points. All points are important, but on certain points it is essential that you not make a careless error. For instance, try to win the first point and get the jump on your opponent. Play steadier on deuce points, or if your opponent gets "tight" (don't let him off the hook). Winning the long rallies is a sign of match toughness and gives you a tremendous psychological advantage. Above all, don't make an error when you find yourself in a long rally.

The first games in each set are important. Don't make the mistake of overhitting with risky shots early in the game or the match, especially when you are playing an opponent you think is better than you. The third point is crucial also. It can keep you from falling behind or it can give you a commanding lead.

As the game nears a climax, apply all the concentration possible on every ball that is hit. Avoid needless errors at 40 − 30, deuce or advantage. This is like the situation of the pitcher with the 3 − 2 count on the batter. Thus, don't gamble on your first serve or on your return.

You		Opponent		7th		Score
5	+	1	+	1	=	6-1
4	+	2	+	1	=	5-2
3	+	3	+	1	=	4-3
2	+	4	+	1	=	3-4
1	+	5	+	1	=	2-5

The seventh game is critical

At the set level, the seventh game is one of the most critical games. The score will be 5 −1, 4 − 2, 3 − all, 2 − 4, or 1 − 5. The winner of the seventh game will probably win the set if he is ahead.

Keeping the Ball Deep

As you play more and encounter better players, you will find that keeping the ball in play is not enough; you must also keep the ball deep.

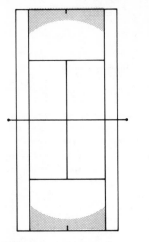

A deep shot lands near the rear of the court

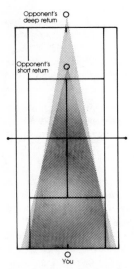

A deep ball reduces the return angle

A deep shot is a ball that lands near the rear of the court. This shot makes it more difficult for your opponent to respond aggressively since:

1. His hitting angle is reduced, which gives you less court to cover than on a short ball.
2. His shot takes longer to get back to you (since it must travel farther), giving you more time to prepare.

These two facts are especially important when you are in trouble and out of position. A deep, floating ball gives you time to recover and to prepare.

For the beginner who has not yet learned to hit the ball safely and with power, a deep ball must clear the net by a good 5 to 8 feet if it is hit from near the baseline. A beginner hitting from a greater distance behind the baseline may even have to hit a lob — a ball that clears the net by more than 8 feet — to keep the shot deep. A more advanced player who hits with more power must clear the net by only 2 or 3 feet on most shots from the baseline. However, the farther behind the baseline you are, the higher you must float the ball back.

The deep, floater ball bounces higher and forces your beginning or intermediate opponent to move substantially back from the baseline to return the ball. This increases the chance of a weak return. For more advanced play, it has value also as a change of pace shot and can be used to slow down a hard-hitting opponent.

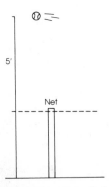

A beginner's floater shot must clear the net by 5' to 8' for depth to result

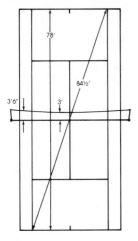

Use a cross-court shot for added safety. Longer court- lower net

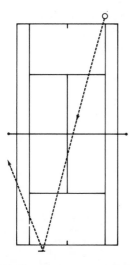

A ball coming cross court tends to ricochet wide off the racket

When to Hit Cross Court

Keeping the ball in play and keeping the ball deep are essential and primary concepts, but they are basically defensive. While thinking defensively and in terms of not making needless errors, you must also be thinking of ways to move your opponent from side to side or up and back. You can either return the ball diagonally across the net (cross court) or parallel to the side line (down the line). There are special considerations for both of these shots.

The cross-court shot, which is almost always a topspin drive, fits well into the strategy we have learned so far. It is a safe beginning shot because:

1. The ball must travel over the center of the net which is 6 inches lower than it is at the sides
2. The court is approximately 5 feet longer diagonally, from one extreme corner to the other, than it is down the line
3. Keeping the ball deep is not so essential. Since a cross-court shot often has sufficient angle to pull your opponent wide, it makes it impossible for him to get into a position to attack.
4. It gives you more margin on a difficult surface or playing in the wind (a down-the-line return of a cross-court shot will tend to ricochet wide off your racket).

Use a cross-court shot:

1. To get your opponent moving. Start the point immediately with a cross-court shot. It makes your opponent run more since it can be hit to greater angles. The more he has to run for a ball, the less chance he has to get set and therefore to transfer his weight into a shot. This increases the chance of a weak return. Even if you are hitting to his strength, a cross-court shot will help to expose his weakness on the next shot.
2. If your opponent hits down the line to you. He will have to move a considerable distance to get to your cross-court return. This gives you an excellent chance to win the point outright (see diagram).

HM MGUINNESS

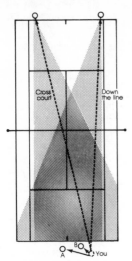

Use a cross-court shot when out of position.

Set position bisects possible angle of return. On a down-the-line shot, recover to point A. Cross court, recover to point B.

3. When you are out of position. You don't have so far to recover in order to bisect the possible angle of return (see diagram).

When to Hit Down the Line

A down-the-line shot is often an underspin shot, such as a slice or chop. It should be used:

1. As a change of routine to the basic cross-court pattern
2. To help get at a player's weakness
3. To hit behind a person running fast to cover the opposite side of the court
4. As the basic attack shot.

Allow more margin for error on the down-the-line shot. Use considerable spin and aim well inside the line, since:

1. The ball travels a shorter distance and over a higher part of the net than a cross-court shot.
2. It is more difficult to follow through the flight of the ball, so the ball tends to slide off the racket to the side.

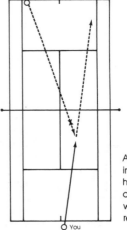

Attack by moving in quickly and hitting forcefully down the line when ball is returned short

When to Hit Short

Basically you want to keep your opponent as far in the backcourt as possible. However, many players don't move forward as well as they move to the side. Also, some players stay in the backcourt because they feel insecure at net. If your opponent never moves up to the net, float a few balls high and deep. If he retreats back to return and his return lands at all short, hit softly and short yourself (a drop shot,

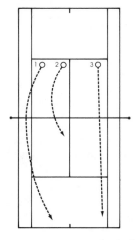

Three ways to play a short ball

1. A defensive floater, allowing time to retreat to the baseline
2. A drop shot to pull your opponent up
3. A hard drive as the first shot in the attack to the net

for instance) to force him to come to the net. Once he gets to the net, try lobbing to him for he may be avoiding the net because of an overhead weakness.

You may also want to return short because your opponent is pulling you to the net and then successfully lobbing or passing you. If you are not effective when you are inadvertently pulled to the net, pull your opponent up by using a soft, short ball (drop shot) instead of an approach shot. Even if this doesn't pull your opponent all the way to the net, short underspin shots following high floaters can be effective change-of-pace shots.

Approaching the Net on a Ground Shot

So far we have discussed mostly defensive tennis. We have seen how basically defensive maneuvers (deep balls or even balls that move your opponent) can force weak or inaccurate returns. When a short ball (weak shot) is hit to you and you must move into the playing court to return it, you may:

1. Play it 100 percent defensively by returning it fairly softly, high, deep, and down the middle — giving your opponent no angle for return and giving yourself time to retreat to a more comfortable position behind the baseline.
2. Play it somewhat defensively by returning it as a drop shot, which tends to pull your opponent up out of position into no-man's-land and gives you time to recover, either back to the baseline or occasionally to the net.
3. Play it 100 percent offensively by approaching the net. Even intermediate players can have reasonable success playing at the net (we have seen how mechanically simple the volley really is) provided they come to net at the right time with the right shot. In other words, the most critical factor in successful net play is the method in getting there — the approach shot itself.

When to Approach the Net You should attempt the approach to the net for any ball that bounces near the serve line (unless it is sharply angled), provided you can be balanced and set in position at the net when the opponent returns. It is wise to approach the net often when playing with a strong wind at your back, since your opponent will have to return into the wind. Don't approach the net on a ball that bounces near your baseline, as you probably will not be able to get close enough to the net to make your first volley effective.

Anticipation of the short ball helps to make your approach shot easier. You must learn to "feel" when the return may be short (the result of a deep, or hard shot, or because the opponent had to run a great distance), and be mentally prepared to move in quickly. Anticipation will get you started a split second sooner, and will allow you time to get to the ball and be balanced and set. (With luck, your opponent will help you by being somewhat out of position for his return of your approach shot.)

How to Approach the Net An inexperienced player will probably come to the net only when chasing a very short ball — when his momentum carries him so far forward he cannot retreat.

A more advanced player will try to set up a short return from his opponent, especially a return to his forehand so he can attack the net himself. Remember, if this is your situation, you have worked the entire rally to get this opportunity. From more steady play, your thoughts must now be immediately changed to "attack" — like the tiger who has worked himself into position to finally "make his kill." At the same time, don't get careless when you finally have the opportunity to attack. Don't overhit — unless you have an obvious opening. Be content to use the approach shot as an interim shot to set up the winning volley. Give yourself plenty of margin.

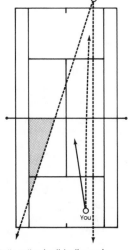

Follow the ball to the net

Cover the down-the-line passing shot. Give your opponent the short cross-court angle (shaded)

Follow the ball to the net. This will help you to bisect the possible angle of return and thus to best cover the return. Depth on the approach shot is critical, since if your opponent is hitting from behind the baseline his cross-court angle for the passing shot is limited and you can therefore prepare yourself for his return down the line.

"Split" to a balanced stop. Hop up so you land momentarily with both feet "split" on the ground as your opponent contacts the ball. It is important that you be completely set when your opponent contacts the ball; don't get caught running headlong forward in an effort to go all the way to the net. Don't come to the net on a ground stroke unless you feel you can get in far enough to cut down effective angle returns and low balls. Be able to change direction by having good balance.

How to Hit the Approach Shot Hit the ball early on the approach. Try to contact the ball no later than at the top of the bounce. This gives your opponent less time to prepare.

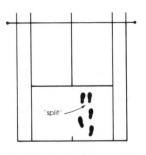

Jump to a "split" stop as your opponent contacts the ball

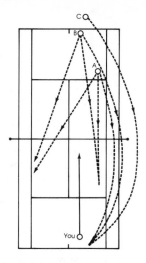

Depth is important on your approach shot

Player A has three good chances to pass you
Player B has a reasonable chance to pass you
Player C can probably only lob

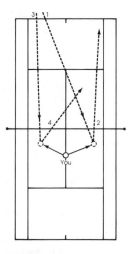

Hit for the opening

If the ball is returned cross court (1) volley down the line (2). If the ball is returned down the line (3), volley cross court (4)

An axiom is that "the earlier a ball is met and the closer you are, the shorter the swing." Most balls taken "on the rise" are hit with an underspin, which requires less backswing, is easier to time, and tends to make the ball bounce low and skid, forcing your opponent to hit up.

Where to Hit the Approach Shot   A more advanced player usually hits down the line on his approach, recognizing that a down-the-line approach shot:

1. Cuts down the court area you must cover on the return. (Cover the down-the-line passing shot first; always give your opponent the short cross-court angle.)
2. Makes it easier to get into position for the volley since you need only move straight ahead to cover the down-the-line return, not all the way over to the other side of the court.

You should concentrate on depth more than speed in your approach shot (unless you have a clear-cut opportunity for a winner), since depth limits your opponent's options for return. A deep shot increases the possibility of a lob or a down-the-line return. (We have already stated it essentially cuts out the chance of a sharp cross-court return.) It is relatively simple for you to cover two possibilities (down the line or the lob), but almost impossible to cover all three (the cross-court as well). Try to keep your return to your opponent's backhand, unless you have a big opening on the forehand side.

How to React to the Return   After "splitting," move forward to the ball and then "set" again to make your shot. Footwork when moving forward is important. Take several small steps into the ball instead of a large, lunging step. An axiom is "if the ball is one step away from you take at least three small quick steps forward to reach it."

Hit for the opening. If the ball is returned down the line, volley cross court. If the ball is returned cross court, volley down the line. If the ball is low, the volley must be deep or very sharply angled. Take the ball as early as possible so it doesn't have time to drop below the level of the net.

If the ball is lobbed very high, let it bounce before hitting for better timing; otherwise always hit on the fly. (Sun and wind may be a factor in letting the ball bounce.) Hit the overhead aggressively from the forecourt (it is a most effective shot in tennis), and play it more defensively (with less swing and power, using some spin) when hitting from deeper in the backcourt.

Approaching the Net after a Serve

Obviously a beginner will rarely use his serve as an attacking weapon. The intermediate player may occasionally come to net on the first serve, but rarely on a second serve. An advanced player may come to net on both the first and second serves as a standard play, especially on faster hard courts and grass, or when serving with the wind at his back. (Don't come to net if you are uncertain about hitting a strong serve. Your opponent can readily exploit your vulnerable position and either pass you outright or force a very weak volley.) A weak serve is made even more ineffective on a slow court such as rough cement or clay, or when serving into a strong wind. In these conditions place less emphasis on attack, especially on a second serve.

You should stay back on your serve if you have been regularly unsuccessful using the serve as an attacking shot (perhaps your opponent has too good a return, or you have been missing many first serves), or to see if your opponent is steady enough to play well in backcourt rallies. If you find yourself down 0 – 30, 0 – 40, or 15 – 40, you may stay back on your serve (and yet perhaps come in on the first short ball, even the return) as a change of pace and to help break your opponent's rhythm.

In any case, you must make up your mind either to go to the net or stay back before you serve. You must not wait to see whether the serve is good or effective.

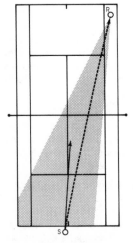

When going to the net as a server, assume a set position that bisects the possible angle of return

To come to net behind the serve, bring your back foot across the baseline into the court on the follow-through of the serve, as the first step in getting to the net. Move forward as rapidly as possible, jumping to a "split" stop at the instant your opponent contacts the return. On a slow serve you will have more time to get closer to the net. Get close to your Home Base at the net as quickly as possible, commensurate with being completely balanced and set when your opponent contacts the return. (Players who don't set well are particularly susceptible to hard returns driven low, and tend to run by the ball).

You should have time for three or four steps before coming to your "split" stop. This puts you in the vicinity of the service line, although probably slightly behind it. You must accept the fact that it is impossible to get all the way to Home Base at the net from behind the baseline on a serve before the ball is returned. Thus, you will have to hit one "approach" shot (volley) from the difficult and relatively vulnerable no-man's-land.

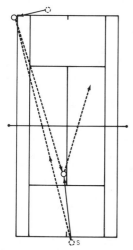

If there is an opening, volley to it

After you "split" stop, move forward with several small, quick steps to the ball where you want to contact it. "Set" again for the volley and try to contact the ball in front of the service line. If the return is down the middle, you are not yet close enough to put any angle on your return so the premium is on volleying deep. If the return is hit wide, you may be able to use more angle on your volley and therefore may not want so much depth.

After you have hit the volley, follow the ball to the net, as when approaching on a ground stroke. Treat the first volley as an approach shot — don't overhit the ball. The first volley should set up your second volley.

If there is an opening, volley to it. For example, a wide serve to the backhand in the backhand (ad) court especially if the ball is returned down the line, leaves the forehand court open. If there is no obvious opening, play the shot conservatively and deep. In fact, many good players volley essentially down the middle of the court in order to cut down the angle for the passing shot.

Defending Against the Net Rusher

Most important in defending against the attack is not to be pressed into trying too good a shot against the net rusher. Don't feel you have only one shot in which to win the point. The axiom is "make your opponent hit the ball to beat you." He does not win the point automatically merely by being at the net. It is remarkable how many "sure" winners are missed at the net. Unless you are confident of hitting an outright winner, use your first shot to pull your opponent out of position, and then be more aggressive on the second shot. Take your time. Don't be rushed into not setting or not staying down with the shot.

The Use of Lobs   The lob is probably the most underused shot in tennis. Occasionally on short balls, especially on down-the-middle balls where little passing angle exists, a quick lob can be effective and actually almost an offensive weapon. Give yourself plenty of margin (never miss a lob wide), and get the ball well up into the air. Any time you are successful in getting a lob over the net player's head, move into the net yourself. Even if the lob doesn't get over the net player's head, it tends to push him away from the net and makes passing shots easier.

Always lob when hitting from substantially behind the base line. Lob often if the sun is a factor, even when not hitting

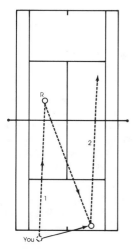

Make your opponent hit the ball to beat you

When passing: Use the first shot (1) to pull your opponent out of position so you can pass him on the second shot (2)

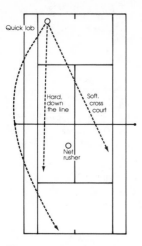

Three choices for the passing
shot hit from within the
base line

from so deep in the backcourt. Although it is difficult to lob in the wind, it is even more difficult to hit an overhead in the wind (don't lob as high when lobbing in the wind).

On hot days, lob extensively early in the match. If the match turns out to be a long one, conditioning could become a determining factor. Lob often on balls that are volleyed deep down the middle, even when returning from near the baseline (you don't have much angle for a passing shot in this situation).

The Use of Passing Shots   The most important principle in the use of passing shots is to keep the ball low, so that if the volleyer reaches the ball he will be forced to hit it up, thus decreasing his opportunity to make an aggressive return shot. Topspin balls drop faster than flat or underspin balls. Therefore, most passing shots are hit with substantial topspin.

The most common passing drives are hit **down the line.** The ball gets to the opponent quickly on a down-the-line shot and gives him little time to prepare. Also it is difficult for a player running to the side to get the racket around the ball fast enough to pass cross court.

Since the net player is probably covering the down-the-line shot, you must hit the ball fairly hard to get it by him. Try to stay forward with the ball as long as you can, almost to the point of letting the forward swing of the racket pull you a step or two into the playing court after the hit. Recover quickly after the shot since the net player will try to volley to the cross-court opening.

The **cross-court** passing shot is a good one if you have the opportunity to hit it, especially when the ball has been volleyed short and low. It is not as important to hit the ball hard, and indeed if your shot is low and soft there is little the volleyer can do. By keeping your ball cross court your opponent has less opening to volley to, leaving you less area to cover in reaching the next shot.

Many times this soft change of pace shot will pull your opponent far enough out of position to set up the passing shot on the next hit. It may also pull him close enough to the net to make him vulnerable to the quick lob.

How to Return a Serve Against the Net Rusher   The basic return is a fairly flat drive, but many net rushers like to volley a hard return and get all tied up when a return comes soft. Use a soft, unspectacular underspin or chip re-

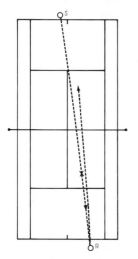

Adjust your receiver's Home Base against a net rusher. For example, stand further back if you are having trouble getting the return in play

turn often, especially against a hard hitter or an extremely fast net rusher. Above all, if you are unsuccessful in returning one way, change and try something different — standing in closer or farther back, hitting softer or harder, hitting for more angle or less angle, or moving in yourself. Play safe, but don't be afraid to "go for it" in a critical situation. Try moving in when your opponent is getting too close to the net for his first volley. You can keep him from getting in so close if you take the ball sooner yourself. Perhaps you can beat him to the net by using the return of service as an approach shot.

Stand farther back than usual if you want more time to react. This also may upset the server's timing as he comes in, since he has to take two or three more steps before he volleys. Keep the ball down the middle to minimize the chance for an angle volley, and be prepared to lob on the second shot.

Practice Drills for the Singles Player

Success in sports is largely due to confidence. Confidence comes from knowing what you can and cannot do well in a specific situation. You can then play within your capabilities.

A systematic effort to turn your weaknesses into strengths will help you gain this confidence. Do a particular thing over and over again until its execution becomes second nature. Start in simple, almost rote, terms, such as "groove" hitting with tossed balls or with a ball machine. Then progress into rallies with a partner, but with sequences that are still definable. Finally, "play the game," where you may have little control over the type and timing of situations that develop.

Although there is some overlap, this section is divided into two types of drills — those for the backcourt player, and those for the net player. A final section incorporates the serve and return.

Backcourt Drills—Groove Hitting (Always hit to a target) With a tossing partner or a ball machine, practice returning:

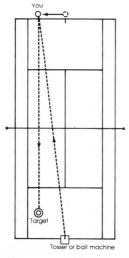

Use a tosser or a ball machine to "groove" hit. Always have a target

1. Wide balls. Start at the center of the court. Turn, by pushing off, and run to where the ball will be. Try to beat the ball to the spot. Emphasize adjusting your steps when you reach the hitting area. Return by skipping back to the

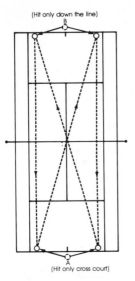

(Hit only down the line)

(Hit only cross court)

Cross-court, down-the-line drill

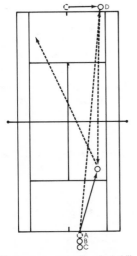

Three-on-one passing shot drill

center of the court. Practice forehands, then backhands. Then alternate forehands and backhands.
2. Short balls and deep balls.

With a hitting partner:

1. Rally cross court (forehand to forehand) or down the line (forehand to backhand). Begin in the service court and move back to full court as your control improves. Emphasize depth when at full court. All balls should land beyond the service line. Try to return to the center mark after each shot.
2. Rally cross court and down the line (Player A hits only cross-court shots, Player B hits only down-the-line shots). Begin in the service court and then move gradually back to the forecourt. Hit three-quarter speed, and don't try to hit too close to the line. The emphasis is on keeping the rally going as long as possible. When you are hurried, put more arc on your return. Try to keep the ball deep (beyond the service line).

Backcourt Drills — Playing   1. Play points. First use the service squares, and then the full court. Practice being steady. Play until one player wins 10 points or until one player makes "two more errors than placements." (Play rally points with every error you make counting as "minus 1" and every placement you make counting as "plus 1." If you commit two more errors than you make placements before your opponent does, you lose the game.) If one player gets pulled to the net, he should hit defensive volleys only. Emphasize changing pace, changing direction, and changing spin.
2. Rally. Begin with a backcourt rally and come in on the first short ball. Either play "points," or play "two more errors than placements."
3. Rally cross court. Both players start in the backcourt. When a short ball is hit, move in and hit the approach shot down the line. The backcourt player tries to pass the net rusher.
4. Play three-on-one passing shots. A, B, and C alternate hitting one ball to D and coming to the net. D hits his passing shot. First all balls are directed to D's forehand, then to his backhand. Finally, Players A, B, and C alternate hitting balls to D's forehand and then to his backhand. Emphasize that Player D always **makes** the shot.

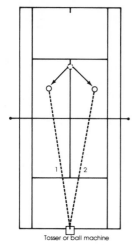

Tosser or ball machine

Alternating forehand and backhand volley drill. (Net player moves diagonally forward to meet ball, then returns to set position)

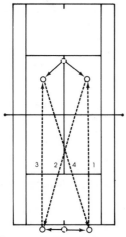

Cross-court, down-the-line drill. One partner at net, the other at the baseline

Net approach drill

Net Player Drills — Groove Hitting   With a tossing partner or a ball machine:

1. Volley wide balls. One player is at the backcourt and Move forward with quick, small steps for the volley and return to your starting position.
2. Alternate wide balls. Hit first a forehand and then a backhand.
3. Practice overheads.

With a hitting partner:

1. Volley wide balls. One player is at the backcourt and the other at the net. Use only one side of the court and return to the center mark each time. The volleyer hits only forehand volleys and hits only to the backcourt player's backhand, or vice versa.
2. Alternate volleys (cross court, down the line). The volleyer hits only cross court, and the backcourt player hits only down the line. Keep the ball in play rather than trying to win the point.
3. Volley rally. Both players are at the net and volley either straight ahead to each other or, standing slightly off-center, diagonally across the court.
4. Practice net approach. Both players start just in front of the baseline. With each shot, both move forward a bit. By the third or fourth shot, both players are at the net in a continuous volley rally.
5. Volley single file. One player is at the net and keeps one ball in play, while four or five other players are in a single-file line. The players follow each other up to the net to hit a volley and then go back to the end of the line. If a shot is missed, another ball is quickly fed to keep the approach rhythm going.

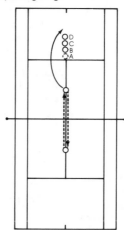

Single file volley approach drill. Use one ball

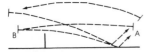

Up-back drill (four-hit overhead
volley drill)

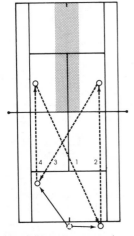

"Aussie" two-on-one passing
shot drill)

Backcourt player keeps
balls out of middle

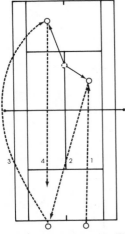

"Aussie" two-on-one net agility
drill

Backcourt players use
many lobs and short shots

6. Practice overheads (Player A back, Player B at net):

  a. Player A lobs, Player B hits overheads.

  b. Up and back: Player A alternates drives and lobs, keeping all balls down the center of the court. Player B moves back for his overhead and then moves quickly in for his volley.

Net Approach Drill — Playing   1. Use one side of the court with one player at the net and one player back. Both players try to win the point, one player by using a combination of lobs and passing shots, the other by using the volley and overhead.

2. Both players play points from the backcourt, but come to net on the first short ball. The point is played to its finish.

3. Practice Australian two-on-one drill. This can be done either with two players at the net and one player back, or one player at the net and the two opponents in the backcourt. In the former case, the net players try to hit the shots so the backcourt player can barely get to them. The backcourt player should not overhit the ball but should try to make each shot simulate a passing shot. He should keep the balls out of the middle and should try to take the short balls as early as he can. In the case of one player at net and his two opponents in the backcourt, the backcourt players try to move the net player around as much as possible and yet hit shots that he conceivably can reach and return.

4. Try the scramble drill. Player A serves and comes to net. Player B has a bucket full of balls. He returns one ball after another to the net rusher for approximately a 12-shot sequence. The object is to make Player A hit his first volley and then move quickly from side to side and up and back for hard drives, lobs, and soft balls. A variation is to start by moving Player A from side to side in the backcourt and then feed him a short ball that takes him to the net so he can work on his approach off the ground rather than off the serve.

Adding the Serve and Return to Practice   Always keep in mind the great importance of practicing all types of serves. Remember also that whenever one person is practicing a serve, someone else can be practicing a return. Practice serving different types of serves to different parts of the court.

1. Practice two-on-one serve and volley (two servers, one receiver). Use second serves only and work on one type of return at a time (such as chip, drive, standing in close, standing back).

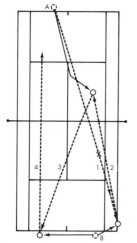

Four-hit drill: Serve and volley, return, and pass

Emphasize making all four shots in sequence — no errors

2. Practice four-hit serve and volley. Player A serves and volleys to the open side of the court. In other words, if the serve is to the ad court, the volley is made to the deuce court. Player B returns so that the server has a chance to volley the ball and then goes for the passing shot.
3. Play points to 10, or until one player makes two more errors than placements.
4. Serve four games or until you are broken (the receiver uses one theme for the entire four-game series — chip or soft returns; drive returns and lob; moves in on second serves, and so on); or serve until you make two errors.

Organize Your Practice Workout   Two or two and one-half hours a day afford enough time for an individual or team to improve at the highest level, provided the time is used wisely. Although time allotment may vary depending on the nearness of competition dates, you cannot go far wrong by spending approximately half of each day's workout in practice (one day for groove hitting, the next day for playing drills) and the other half in playing (points, games, or sets; alternating singles and doubles). Drills should be selected from the previous section to provide isolated work on backcourt play (ground strokes), net play, serving, and receiving. A brief prepractice warm-up period may include some jogging as well as body stretching. At the conclusion of practice, a 15-minute conditioning period may include sit-ups, push-ups, jumping rope, sprints, and agility drills. A sample five-day workout schedule follows on page 66.

MORE ADVANCED DOUBLES STRATEGY

Doubles is an exciting and fast-moving game that requires great teamwork and communication between partners. You should keep this in mind in choosing a partner, and you should also give consideration to choosing a partner whose style of play might complement your own. (Often a quick touch player and a slower but more powerful partner form a good team.)

Although the court is 9 feet wider in doubles play than in singles, two players can cover the entire area with comparative ease. Unlike singles, then, the probability is low that you will be able to maneuver your opponents out of position when you are hitting from the backcourt: the angle to which to hit is just too limited. It is also unlikely you will

A Sample Five-day Workout Schedule

Time	Drill	Monday	Tuesday	Wednesday	Thursday	Friday
2:00	Warm-up	Warm-up (jogging, stretching)	Warm-up (jogging, stretching)	Warm-up (jogging, stretching)	Warm-up (jogging, stretching)	Warm-up (jogging, stretching)
2:15	Serve, Return	Serve, return	Serve, return	Serve, return	Serve, return	Serve, return
2:30	Ground Strokes	Grooving (partner or ball machine)	Aussie Two-on-One (passing shot)	1) Cross Court/Down the Line 2) Cross-court rally – attack on short ball	Points from Backcourt (come in on short ball)	Grooving (partner or ball machine)
3:00	Net Play	1) Cross Court/Down the Line (one up, one back) 2) Overheads	Grooving (partner or ball machine)	1) Overheads 2) Up-Back (four-hit cycle)	1) Net Approach Drill (both partners start at baseline) 2) Volley Rally	Aussie Two-on-One (net agility drill)
3:30	Play	Singles (sets)	Doubles	Singles (points/games)	Doubles	Singles (sets)
4:15	Conditioning	Conditioning	Conditioning	Conditioning	Conditioning	Conditioning

be able to use power as effectively from the backcourt — it is difficult to hit "through" two opponents from a backcourt position.

These two considerations dictate advanced doubles strategy: get to the net where angles do exist and where quickness and touch can do some good. Since the court is easier to cover, both partners can get to the net with less risk than in singles. Even in beginning doubles, you and your partner should attempt to position yourselves at the net. Both the server's partner and the receiver's partner begin the point at the net, and both the server and the receiver should attempt to join their partners there as soon as possible. Once at the net, the prime goal is to make your opponents hit up to you so you can move in and hit down. Proper court position is the most important factor in successful doubles at the beginning and at least through the intermediate level. Basic positions have already been covered. Now the goals of each team and specific situations will be discussed.

Strategy for the Serving Team

Who Should Serve First?   Usually the best server should serve first in each set. Sometimes a special playing condition, such as a tail wind or absence of sun glare, will favor beginning with the weaker server (neither server should have to serve into the sun if one is left-handed and one is right-handed).

Get the First Serve In   Fewer chances should be taken with the first serve in doubles and more margin should be allowed (more spin, for example) to get the ball in play. A good first serve is of great importance, because:

1. Your partner at the net can poach more effectively.
2. As the server, you can come to the net more readily. An intermediate player should come to net on many first serves, but much less often on second serves. An advanced player will regularly come to net on both serves, since the majority of points can be won by the team who gets to the net first.
3. You have the strategic advantage. If you miss the first serve, the receiver will probably have an easier return on your second serve. You usually hit your second serve with less pace and more spin, which gives it a tendency to land short. Also, you can take fewer chances on the second serve. The receiver knows it will probably be served to his backhand and he can gamble — run around his backhand, move in quicker, and so on.

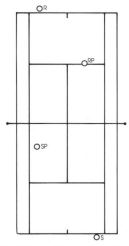

Starting position for doubles. Join your partner at the net when:

1. You hit a strong serve (get your first serve in)
2. You can return serve effectively
   If you can't come to net on the serve or return, come to net on the next opportunity:

   a) A short ball
   b) A short lob to your partner at net
   c) A lob over the opposing net player's head

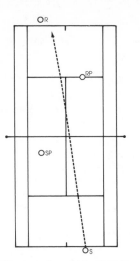

The down-the-middle serve is the basic serve to the deuce court. The down-the-middle serve:

1. Cuts down the return angle
2. Is an easy serve on which to poach

Serve Wide   The most effective wide serves are the slice to the forehand in the deuce court, and the twist to the backhand in the ad court. The wide serve can be effective if:

1. Your opponent is getting to the net off the return too quickly. A wide serve slows him down by moving him wide for the return instead of letting him move forward.
2. Your opponent has trouble returning a wide shot.
3. Both opponents are behind the base line. This tends to pull the receiver wide, opening up the court for approach by the server's partner.

Serve to the Middle   The serve to the middle of the court is the basic serve to backhand in the deuce court. The ball served to the center of the court makes it easier for the server's partner to poach toward the center since it is more difficult for the opponent to return the angle to the alley. For this reason the server's partner at the net will often begin the point standing closer to the center of the court in the deuce court since the basic serve is to the backhand (middle of the court). In the ad court, the serve will probably be wide, so the partner will often stand closer to the alley.

This serve to the ad court is effective when:

1. Your opponent is "keying" for the usual serve to his backhand, especially on an "ad" point.
2. Your opponent overswings regularly on his forehand return. This ball can be served in tight to cramp his swing.
3. The receiver has a good angle return. This cuts down his return angle.

The Poach   Poaching is a service strategy in which the net player moves toward his partner's side of the court to intercept a return shot. The net player should always move diagonally forward on the poach to take the ball as close to the net as possible. The poaching net player aims his return shot at the opening between the receiver, who is back, and the net player, or slightly toward the net player's feet. If the poaching player's momentum carries him to the server's side of the court, the serving partner moves over to cover the poacher's original side.

If the serving team decides to poach often in a particular match, it may be advantageous for the net player to signal his intentions in advance to his partner. He may signal either a stay, a poach, or a fake poach. The decision to poach now becomes an all-or-nothing commitment. The server

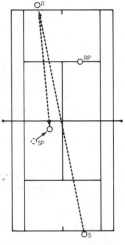

The poacher always moves diagonally forward

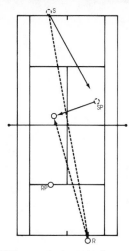

If the poacher's momentum carries him across the center of the court, the server must cross to cover the open side

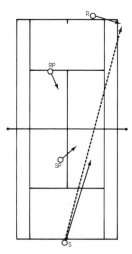

Use Australian doubles to:

1. Break up the rhythm of the receiver
2. Test the receiver to see if he can return as well down the line
3. Cover up a volley weakness of the server, or make the receiver return to a volley strength. (As shown above, the server would only have to hit forehand first volleys)

must cover his partner's side immediately upon serving if the poach signal has been given.

If you are the server in a poaching situation, serve from a position closer to the center of the court. In order to protect against the angle return serve more down the middle. The poach stands the best chance of being effective on the first serve, so concentrate on getting the first serve in and don't try a risky serve.

The poach is a good move:

1. If you are having trouble winning the point serving to a particular side of the court. In this case the poach can break the receiver's rhythm and keep him from grooving his return. The receiver has many more things to think about against a poaching net player.
2. On a big point, such as "ad out." Here the poach can help the server out of a jam, especially if he has had to struggle to win his serve.
3. If the serve is deep. If the ball lands near the serve line be ready to move.
4. If the return is a floating underspin. This shot often lends itself to poaching.

Play "Australian" Doubles Another service strategy to counteract an effective return (specifically the wide-angle return on the backhand from the ad court) is to position the server's partner on the same side of the court as the server, where he can intercept the cross-court return. The server must serve from close to the center of the court so he can move over to the opposite side to cover the territory usually covered by his partner.

If the server is serving to the ad court, the net player starts at the net on the left (instead of the right) side of the court. The server serves from the left side near the center, and moves to the right side to continue the point. This forces the receiver to return down the line, often a difficult return for the player with a good cross-court backhand. The maneuver may be tried on certain points to break the receiver's rhythm or to help get out of a particular jam.

The server's partner may opt to poach from his "center of the court position." In this case, it is an especially good idea for him to use signals to let his partner know his intention before the serve. Also, if the server has an especially good volley on one side or is weak on the other, a team may use Australian doubles. For example, if Australian doubles is used when serving into the ad court, the server should never

have to hit a backhand volley since he will be moving toward the forehand side of the court.

Usually Australian doubles will not be employed on a second serve, since the receiver will anticipate a serve to the backhand side of the court and can run around it and hit a forehand return using maximum angle.

Strategy for the Receiving Team

Who Returns from which Court?   In determining who receives the first point (which partner receives on the deuce court and which on the ad court) the prime consideration should be, Where does each receiver feel more comfortable? Usually a player with a natural underspin backhand will play the deuce (forehand) court, where most serves are in close to the receiver's backhand. The partner with the better drive backhand (topspin) usually plays the ad (backhand) court, since there is more room on this side for a fuller return swing.

A left-handed player may play the ad court to keep the server serving down the middle, and to keep both partners' forehands on the outside where more reach is needed. Or, the left-hander may play the deuce court to keep both forehands in the middle where most balls are hit.

The stronger player may play the deuce court, where more points (at least half) are served (the ad receiver returns one less point in a 40 – 15 game, for example). Or the stronger player may play the ad court because he is better able to handle the pressure at "game" point.

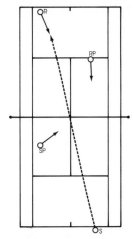

The chip is generally the most effective return against the net rusher for the ball is taken early, thus 1) giving the opposing net player less time to poach, 2) giving the server less time to get to net

Hitting the Return A good return of serve is one of the most important shots in doubles, for it sets the tempo of the point. In advanced doubles the receiver assumes the server is coming to the net and his goal is to keep the ball low to the approaching server in order to make him volley up. The receiver will usually come to net on the return of serve also, although the first rule is get the ball in play.

As an advanced receiver, adjust your court position so that you have the best chance to get the ball in play. Move back a little if you are having difficulty in returning a hard serve. The farther back you stand, the more you can swing and drive the return (more topspin). The closer in you stand, the more you must shorten your swing and block or chip the return (more underspin). This also gives you a better chance to protect against the poach, to hit down on the return, and to move in to volley.

Against a poaching team, use a chip lob often to get the ball quickly over the poaching net player's head. If a team is known to poach often, start the match by hitting behind the poacher early so that your opponents will know you are not afraid to do it. If this still doesn't work, start the point with both partners on the base line.

Against Australian doubles, take the ball early and hit down the line or chip lob over the net player's head. If the team goes Australian on the second serve, you know it will probably be served to your backhand, so run around it and crack a forehand.

The Receiver's Partner If you are the receiver's partner you normally begin on the center of the service line. Your responsibility is to call the out serves and watch your partner's return. If the return is reasonably low and to the approaching server, move forward into a position about 10 feet from the net. If the return goes toward the net player (either because of a poor return or a poach) move back and toward the center to give yourself time to react and to cut off the opening in the middle of the court. If the return serve is low and to the center of the court, you can poach to the center.

Standing Back As the receiver's partner, you may choose to stand back at the baseline if:

1. The server's partner is poaching often (on first serves, for example) and effectively. The poacher is less able to hit an outright winner at your feet and between partners if you are back.

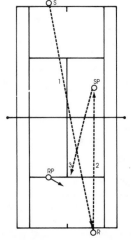

If the serve is returned to the net player, the receiver's partner drops back toward the center to cover the middle

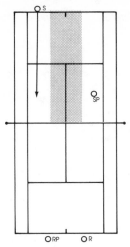

Positions for "standing back"

Keep balls down the middle (shaded area) to reduce angle returns

2. Your partner is having particular trouble with his return. With both partners back, the receiver has more margin for his return — the low return is not so critical and the receiver can just concentrate on getting the ball back.
3. The server is consistently beating the receiver to the net and by better positioning is winning the point on his first volley. (Play from the backcourt requires a less exacting return, and makes it more difficult for the opposing server to put the first volley away for the winner.)
4. The serving team is a "groove" team and has established a fast pace and momentum. The receiving team should stay back and try to break the momentum. This can also be effective as a psychological maneuver on select points, such as the first two points of a game, if the serving team has been holding serve rather easily on the first part of the set.
5. You want to exploit an opponent's weak overhead or a weak partner. In this situation, the receiver and his partner stand substantially back and just try to get the ball in play on the return. Once it is in play, try to keep hitting to one partner and alternate drives and deep lobs to make him move up and back. If there is a short ball, then both you and your partner go to the net.

Strategy When Both Teams Are at the Net

The great majority (75 percent) of all points in advanced doubles end with all four players at the net, like in-fighting in boxing. While both teams are waiting for an offensive opportunity, the emphasis is on keeping the ball low. This often requires softer shots. Once one team hits the ball up, however, the opposing team moves in for the knockout punch.

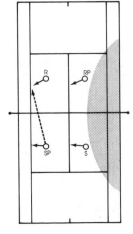

Player's move toward the side of the court the ball is on. Most balls should be kept down the middle, for a wide ball opens up part of the court (shaded area)

Down-the-Middle Balls   Most balls are hit down the middle when all four players are at the net. If you are moving in when a ball is returned down the middle, you should probably take the ball. If you have been pulled wide, your partner must move over and cover the middle. If your opponents are returning the wide ball, the partner on that side must cover the alley while his partner covers the center. If neither player is moving, the player with the forehand in the middle will usually take the shot. If there is any doubt, go for the ball. Above all, don't be indecisive.

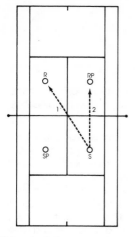

1) Low balls should be returned softly to the feet of the farther player

2) High balls should be smashed at the feet of the nearest player

Low Balls Return the low ball to the feet of the player farther from you. This cross-court volley gives the ball more time to drop to your opponent's feet. If you are successful in returning low, move in close, for your opponent must volley up and you will then be in a good position to volley down for the winner. Be aggressive and keep attacking. The farther back you stand, the easier it is for your opponents to hit to your feet. Try an extreme angle shot only if you can probably hit for an outright winner. Don't give your opponents an angle return.

High Balls If the ball is returned up to you, move in quickly and hit down at the feet of the opponent nearer to you. Anticipate the high ball by virtue of your low return. Start closing in even before your opponent hits the low return. The partner who is not hitting is ready to back up the hitting player in case the opponents try a quick lob or lob volley. (The lob volley is a difficult shot, however, and will not often be successful.)

Strategy When You Are at the Net and Your Opponents Are Back

Be Patient Realize the rallies will be longer and it will be harder to put the ball away. Don't try to power the ball past your opponents. Short, angled volleys can be effective since they tend to pull one partner up and out of position. **But** if you don't have enough angle to win the point outright, keep the ball deep and down the middle. This will keep your opponents back on defense.

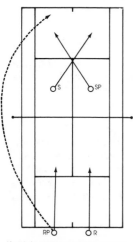

If a lob gets over your head, both partners move back. Return with a lob since your opponents will be moving in.

If the lob goes over the server's head, the server's partner will often cross to take the return since he has a better hitting angle. In this case, the server crosses to cover the vacant side of the court

Expect the Lob Play farther from the net: 15 feet away is not too far back if you don't have much confidence in your overhead. Let the really high lobs bounce, but try not to let other lobs get over your head. If the lob should get over one player's head, both partners retreat back. Since your opponents will be moving in, the competitive return is a high defensive lob.

If you are hitting the overhead from deep in your court, hit with more spin and less power, and hit it more down the middle. Smash all short lobs and high balls hard and down the middle unless you have a tremendous angle. When both opponents are back you have a great chance to play the weaker player.

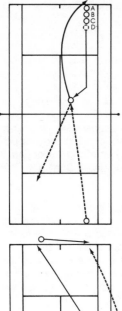

Practice Drills for Doubles Players

Single-File Drill   Four players stand in single file just inside the baseline and the alley. One player is on the other side of the net.

1. The poach. One player at a time comes in and split stops from the starting position. The ball is hit toward the center of the court and the volleyer moves diagonally forward to volley it. He then returns to the back of the line.
2. The lob. Two players from the line take positions as partners. The player on the opposite side of the net lobs. If the lob is short the net player hits the overhead, if it is deep, the net player yells "switch" and crosses and goes back. His partner crosses deep and lobs the ball back.

Six-Player Volley   Three players are on each side of the net. The middle player on one side has a bucket of balls and starts the rally. The volley rally continues, with each of the six players ready to hit by turning to face where each ball is coming from. Players should be careful not to over-anticipate the shot.

The Two-Player Doubles Attack   Play full speed attacking points but with only two players. This drill develops soft volleys to set up the put-away. It illustrates the importance of getting to the net quickly. All balls must be hit to the court diagonally opposite you. Both the server and the receiver come in. Use only second serves so as to get more balls in play.

Practice Situations   It is important not only to practice drills but to practice situations, especially the ones you will have to adapt to in certain conditions and certain matches. Practice both as the serving team and as the receiving team in (a) Australian doubles, and (b) with the receiving team staying in the back court.

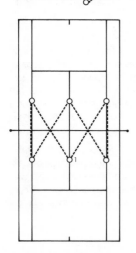

Single-file poach drill (top)

Single-file lob drill (middle)

Six-player volley rally (use one ball) (bottom)

BACKGROUND OF TENNIS

HISTORY

Tennis has a rich and intriguing background. Its history has been marred by misfortune, but even kings could not prevent its rise in popularity. The development of tennis equipment, facilities, and methods has made modern tennis one of the world's most interesting sports.

Tennis is a derivative of a game similar to handball which was played in ancient Greece, Rome, Egypt, Persia, and Arabia. A wandering minstrel is thought to have introduced the game to Europe — to the ladies and noblemen of the French court. The game was played indoors, with a rope cord stretched across the room to serve as a net, or outdoors, across a mound of dirt. At first, the open hand was used to bat a cloth bag stuffed with hair back and forth. Later, an all-wood racket, similar to a large ping-pong paddle, was used.

Although in the 10th century Louis IV banned tennis as undignified, it continued to grow in popularity. Louis X again outlawed it, in the 1300s, because he felt "tennis should be thought of as a 'Sport for Kings.'"

In 13th and 14th century France, tennis was known as "jeu de paume" or "sport of the hands." However, its current name is probably derived from the French word "tenez," meaning "take it" or "plan."

In the 14th century, the game moved to England, but there, too, it had a dubious beginning. It was outlawed because the king felt his soldiers wasted the time playing tennis that they could have spent practicing archery.

Tennis was played very little for the next 200 years. Interest slowly revived in France, England, and other European countries in the 16th century. A net replaced the rope cord, and a racket shaped like a snowshoe, with gut strings, was developed. Tennis became a more competitive game, and it was common to wager on the outcome of matches.

Edicts were published to ban tennis, this time because of the betting, and the sport again declined in popularity until, by the 19th century, only the wealthy were playing the game.

The modern history of tennis began in 1873, when Major Walter Wingfield introduced lawn tennis in England. His was a 15-point game in which only the server could score. Called "sphairistike" after the Greek root for "ball," it was played on an hourglass-shaped court divided by a net 7 feet high.

Mary Outerbridge introduced tennis to the United States in 1874. A Bermuda vacation gave her the opportunity to see British soldiers, friends of Wingfield, playing "sphairistike," and, in spite of initial difficulty with United States customs officials, she succeeded in bringing two rackets, a ball, and a net into this country. She was largely responsible for establishing the first court in the United States, on the lawn of the Staten Island Cricket and Baseball Club.

The sport caught on quickly and developed into a vigorous, fast-moving game of skill. In 1881, the United States Lawn Tennis Association was founded to standardize rules pertaining to scoring, size of the ball and racket, and court dimensions. Today, individual players, schools, recreation departments, cities, and clubs belong to the USTA and the popularity of tennis continues to grow.

JIM M°GUINNESS

COMPETITION

Tennis is in a state of flux today. Until recently, tournaments of any consequence were open only to amateurs (players ineligible to receive prize money). The limited number of professionals (usually the best one or two amateurs each year "turned pro" in order to play for money) played mostly barnstorming exhibition matches throughout the world. Tournaments, in order to secure the best players, paid so much "under the table" to attract the top amateurs that many amateurs were actually making more money than the pros. In an effort to end this hypocrisy, the British, in 1968, made the most important tournament in the world — Wimbledon, held first in 1877 — an event open to both amateurs and professionals, and offered prize money. The result has been that all major international tournaments are now open to both professionals and amateurs (mostly college students and younger, ineligible for prize money). Another major development has been an increase in the number of major tournaments being played indoors, which has truly made tennis a year-round sport for both spectators and players.

Major World Team Competitions

Davis Cup winners:

Australia
Britain
France
Italy
South Africa
Sweden
United States

Davis Cup (Established in 1900)   For this competition, each country annually sends its top male players to compete in dual matches against countries in the same zone. Then the zone winners play off. Through 1971, the eventual winner earned the right to "challenge" the previous year's championship country in the Challenge Round, but the Challenge Round concept has been abolished. Each round of play consists of four singles matches and one doubles match.

Wightman Cup (Established in 1923)   This trophy is awarded annually to the winner of a dual match between British and American women. Play consists of five singles and two doubles matches.

Federation Cup (Established in 1963)   The International Lawn Tennis Federation initiated this international team competition for women, in which one nation plays another (two singles, one doubles) in a single elimination tournament at one site in one week.

The World Cup (Established in 1969)   The top United States men play a dual match of five singles and two doubles against another country. Since its inception, the World Cup has been played against Australia.

World team tennis match format

1. One set each of:
   Men's singles
   Women's singles
   Men's doubles
   Women's doubles
   Mixed doubles

2. No ad scoring is used

3. The total number of games won by a team determines the over-all match winner

World Team Tennis (Established in 1974)   Professional tennis has attempted to become a factor in the team or league sports market. It is different from most other sports in that its player draft is more international and includes both men and women. Professional tennis has been confined to several cities that have teams in the United States. However, in 1977, a Russian team entered the competition and a European Division is soon to be established.

Major Individual Competitions

The top international tournaments (now all "open" events) are the All-England Championships (Wimbledon), the United States Championships (recently moved from Forest Hills to Flushing Meadows, New York), the French Championships, and the Australian Championships (although the Australian championships are of decreasing importance). Play consists of single elimination type competition. The only players to have completed a "Grand Slam" by winning all four tournaments in the same year are Don Budge and Maureen Connolly of the United States, and Rod Laver (two times) and Margaret Smith Court of Australia.
Three major adult circuits are:

Virginia Slims (Established in 1970)   This is a circuit of professional women players which continues almost weekly throughout the first half of the calendar year. There are "Futures" Satellite tournaments for qualification, and at the conclusion of the circuit the top performers play off for bonus money in a special event.

World Championship Tennis (Established in 1971)   Many of the top men of the world play in a series of weekly tournaments during the first third of the calendar year. These tournaments are very selective.

The Grand Prix (Established in 1970)   This started as a male circuit for a part of the calendar year. Now it has evolved into a year-round circuit of male and female players. It includes major designated tournaments each week in more than half the weeks of the calendar year. It includes the "Grand Slam" tournaments and several of the World Championship of Tennis events. Cumulative points are awarded for performance throughout the circuit. The governing body — the Men's International Professional Tennis Council — administers these tournaments. One or two other lesser events in terms of prize money are held simultaneously in any one week with a major tournament.

ADMINISTRATIVE STRUCTURE

The United States Tennis Association (USTA)
51 E. 42nd Street, New York, N.Y. 10017, 212–953–1020

The United States is divided into 17 sections, all governed by the United States Tennis Association, but each responsible for promoting and governing tennis competition in its own geographic area. Groupings in local and national competition are by age and sex: youths, under 12, 14, 15, 18, and 21; men's, over 35, 50, 55, 60, 65, 70, and 75; and women's, over 35, 45, 50, and 55. All play singles or doubles. Competition also exists in mixed doubles.

Youths may enter a specific age group only if they have not reached the maximum age in that group by October 1 of the year of competition. An adult may play in an age group if he reaches the minimum age any time in the year of competition.

USTA Sections

Eastern	ETA, P.O. Box 925, Mamaroneck, NY 10543
Florida	FTA, 520 Northeast 118th St., Biscayne Park, FL 33161
Hawaii	Larry Eichworth, Diamond Head Tennis Center, 3908 Paki Ave., Honolulu, HI 96815
Intermountain	Gil Roberts, P.O. Box 6740, Denver, CO 80206
Middle Atlantic	Unni MacDonald, 5656 Ravenel Lane, Springfield, VA 22151
Middle States	MSTA, 3 Club Lane, Reading, PA 19607
Missouri Valley	Carl Simonie, 10407 Walrond, Kansas City, MO 64137
New England	NELTA, P.O. Box 223, Needham, MA 02192, 617-444-1332
Northern California	NCTA, P.O. Box 337, Moraga, CA 94556, 415-376-7320
Northwestern	Mrs. Rosemary Rockwell, 3769 Towndale Dr., Bloomington, MN 55431
Pacific Northwest	Mr. Harold Parrot, P.O. Box 130, Gresham, OR 97030
Puerto Rico	Mrs. Lydia de la Rosa, P.O. Box 40456, Minillas Station, Santurce, PR 00940
Southern California	SCTA, 609 North Cahuenga Blvd., Los Angeles, CA 90004, 213-467-5151
Southern	STA, 3121 Maple Drive, N.E., Room 21-B, Atlanta, GA 30305, 404-237-1319
Southwestern	Kenneth Tannenbaum, 405 Lawyers Title Bldg., Tucson, AZ 85701
Texas	TTA, P.O. Box 192, Austin, TX 78767
Western	WTA, 1024 Torrence Drive, Springfield, OH 45503, 513-390-2740

Each section has almost weekly competition in most events during the season of play — which means almost the entire year in some climates. Regular "circuits" of play are established within and between sections, and local and national rankings in each category are published yearly. Information regarding competition opportunities can be obtained from each section's headquarters.

The International Lawn Tennis Federation (ILTF)

Barons Court, W. Kensington, London, W.14, England

The governing body of international tennis is the International Lawn Tennis Federation. This federation establishes the rules of tennis, and the United States Tennis Association is a member of this organization.

The Association of Tennis Professionals (ATP)

P.O. Box 58144, World Trade Center, Dallas, Texas 75258, 214-747-9948

Most of the top playing professionals in the world belong to this association, which has been instrumental in establishing guidelines for the professional tournament circuit and for the conduct of its members. It is an increasing force in the world of tennis and represents one of the first attempts by the players themselves to govern their play. Formerly they were governed by the amateur organization, the USTA.

U.S. Professional Tennis Association, Inc. (USPTA)

6701 Highway 58, Harrison, Tenn. 37341, 615-344-8397

This is an organization of U.S. teaching professionals. One of its main goals is the upgrading of the quality of teaching in the United States at the professional level.

USTA Education and Research Committee

71 University Place, Princeton, N.J. 08540, 609-924-4343

This organization works to upgrade all levels of teaching in the United States. Updated lists of publications and films can be obtained from this committee.

PUBLICATIONS

International Tennis Weekly

P.O. Box 58085, World Trade Center
Dallas, Texas 75258

(The official publication of the ATP)
Published weekly by the ATP

Tennis Magazine

495 Westport Avenue, Norwalk, Connecticut 06856,
203–847–5811

(The official publication of the USPTA)
Published monthly by Tennis Features, Inc.

Tennis, USA Magazine

Chilton Way, Radnor, Pennsylvania 19089

(The official publication of the USTA)
Published monthly by Chilton Company

USTA Yearbook

156 Broad Street, Lynn, Massachusetts 01901

Published annually by H.O. Zimman, Inc.

Contains complete tennis rules, USTA age group rankings
and championship results, and historical results of world's
top events.

World Tennis Magazine

383 Madison Avenue, New York, N.Y. 10017

Published monthly by CBS Publications

EQUIPMENT

Racket

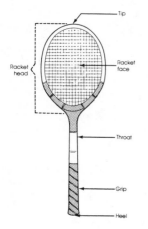

Racket head
Tip
Racket face
Throat
Grip
Heel

Wood vs. Metal   Until the last decade rackets were primarily made of wood. A wood racket consists of many high-grade pieces of wood, put together with glue, heat, and pressure. The racket head is made of plied strips of ash and fiber. The outside strips are often composed of hardwood, such as bamboo. The throat is made of a hardwood such as maple or birch. The laminations, up to 11 in a good racket, give it added strength.

Now there are many new rackets on the market using various materials—fiberglass, graphite, steel, etc.

There is quite a difference in how various rackets play, especially in their flexibility or stiffness. If you are thinking of purchasing an expensive racket, if possible try it out first. Whether to buy a wood or metal racket, though, is mostly a matter of personal preference and has nothing to do with the ability of the player.

Weight   The weight of a racket is something that individual preference should control. It is best to choose the racket that feels most comfortable to you. A general guide is:

> Light weight: 12-13 ounces (girls and women)
> Medium weight: 13½-13¾ ounces (boys and most men)
> Heavy weight: 14-15 ounces (some men)

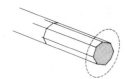

Circumference of handle

Handle Size (grip)   The size of the grip is measured by the circumference of the handle. This, along with the general weight classification, is usually marked on the racket by the manufacturer. You should choose the grip that feels most comfortable. A general guide is:

> 4¼-4½ inches: young children and women
> 4½-4⅝ inches: boys and some women
> 4⅝-4¾ inches: men

Balance   Most rackets are evenly balanced. In a 27″ racket (the most common length) the balance point is 13½″ from the end of the racket. Most people now prefer a racket rather light in the head, because it helps their touch when volleying. A player who spends much time at the baseline may prefer a racket slightly heavy in the head, since it tends to afford more power.

Standard string thickness.
15-gauge

Tournament thickness
16-gauge

Strings   Nylon is relatively durable and cheap ($6–12). Gut provides a better feel, but is more expensive ($12–25) and can be adversely affected by moisture. Generally, gut is strung to 55–65 pounds tension, as opposed to nylon's 45–55 pounds. Some players feel the more flexible the racket frame, the less tightly the racket should be strung.

To $10 — Beginning with young child only; won't last with hard hitting.

$15-20 — Fair frame with nylon strings; beginning youth or adult.

$25-30 — Good wood frame and good nylon strings or cheap gut, intermediate youth or adult.

$30 up — Best wood and gut; tournament players. (Metal frames start around $30 without strings.)

The standard string thickness is 15-gauge but tournament players generally prefer a thinner (16-gauge) string, which wears more rapidly but affords more feel. Individual strings may usually be replaced at a nominal cost.

Cost   There is a great range in racket price. The most expensive racket is not necessarily the best for you. Rackets cost from $10 to over $50. A serious beginner should purchase a medium grade racket, prestrung with a medium grade nylon, for $20 to $25. An intermediate or advanced adult who is serious about tennis should probably not spend less than $20 for a racket frame (without strings).

Care   Metal rackets cost more but tend to last longer and require virtually no care. The use of laminations has greatly reduced the need for special care of a wood racket, but it should be kept in a press if it is subjected to much moisture or if it is to be stored for a long period.

The press protects a wood racquet from warping

A layer of adhesive tape around the edge of the wood racket head can help to keep exposed strings from wear caused by contact of the racket with the ground.

Balls

Tennis balls are made of rubber molded into two cups which are cemented together and covered with wool felt. Some balls are covered with extra felt for increased wear and are called "heavy duty" balls. The heavy duty balls are best on courts not having too rough a surface (which causes them to fluff up), and at higher altitudes. The best balls are inflated with compressed air or gas which gives them their resiliency. Some balls now receive at least some of their resiliency from the rubber that is used.

Specifications   The official ball is approximately 2½ inches in diameter and weighs 2 ounces. It should bounce approximately 55 inches when dropped from 100 inches.

Care   The ball can should not be opened until ready for use, since it is pressure-sealed to help retain the pressure within the ball. Even when kept in an unopened can for an excessive period, a ball's compression is gradually reduced and the ball tends to "deaden." Commercial "compressor" cans are now available.

The felt of a good ball will wear, making the ball considerably lighter after two or three hard sets. For this reason, balls are changed every nine games or so in a championship tournament. For noncompetitive play, however, the life of an otherwise good ball may be temporarily restored by putting the ball through a cycle in a clothes washer and dryer.

Dress

Until recently, the traditional tennis costume was all white, mainly because white reflects heat better than other colors. However, tennis fashion is now a big business, and colors and coordinated outfits are commonplace. Men wear shorts, shirt (always), tennis shoes, sweater or jacket, or warm-up suit, socks, cap, and wrist band (perspiration absorbent and worn by top players to help keep perspiration from eyes and hands). Women wear the same, except that most women favor a blouse and shorts or a tennis dress.

JIM M'GUINNESS

TYPES OF COURT

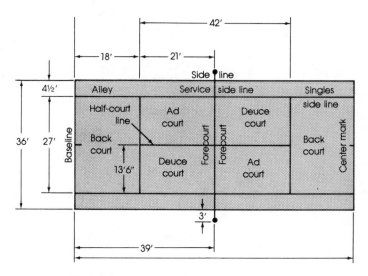

Court diagram

The type of court is largely determined by the climate and traditions of a particular location. The court may be indoors or outdoors, and may be grass, soft court ("clay"), or hard court. A canvas, "plastic" saran, hedge, or wooden slat "fencing" often surrounds the court to reduce the wind and increase visibility of the ball.

Grass Courts

Grass provides a popular traditional court surface, a carryover from the early days of the game when people erected a net and played on their estates.

Today it is the world's least common surface, though the Wimbledon and Australian Championships are still played on grass. Most of the grass courts in the United States are located in the East.

Advantages Most players enjoy playing on a grass court. The style of play is more aggressive than on clay, as the ball tends to skid and bounce low. The grass surface encourages net play, largely because of the ever-present possibility of bad bounces.

Disadvantages Grass courts require constant maintenance. The grass must be clipped smooth and kept watered, and the lines need frequent remarking. When the courts are damp, the ball becomes heavy and wet. The courts can be slippery. Where the turf is worn, bounces become irregular and unpredictable, and most touring professionals become impatient with a surface that can be so imperfect.

Soft Courts

In areas where grass doesn't grow well, or where it is difficult to secure composition materials, dirt or clay is a common court surface. Most of the world's tennis courts are classified as "soft" courts and are a clay-like material. This is by far the most common European surface. In the United States, the South, Midwest and East have a high proportion of clay courts.

Advantages Clay courts are easy on the feet. The style of play is slightly slower, and less emphasis is placed on attack. The ball bounces higher and more slowly off the rough surface, so the player has more time to run and prepare for his shot.

Disadvantages The clay court is difficult to keep in top playing condition. It must be watered and rolled daily, the chalk lines need remarking regularly, or tape lines need to be swept or reset.

Court and fencing

Hard Courts

Courts surfaced with asphalt, cement, wood, composition materials, or carpets are classified as hard courts. Internationally, this is the least common surface. It is essentially the only type of court in the western United States, however.

Advantages   The ball bounces uniformly. A minimum of upkeep is required, although an asphalt court should be resurfaced every four or five years. The courts often are painted to facilitate visibility, usually a green court bordered by a red area surrounding the playing lines.

Disadvantages   The primary disadvantage is that this is not the standard court throughout the world. Some people object to the aggressive type of play possible on the faster court because the ball rebounds so quickly from the playing surface.

Indoor Tennis

The rapid rise of indoor facilities in the United States has made tennis a year-round activity for the first time in many areas. Rented court time has made many indoor centers commercially attractive. In addition, major indoor competitive circuits have evolved. Much indoor play is on a carpet surface.

United States	82%
Australia	25%
England	15%
Germany	5%

Percent of hard courts in several leading tennis countries

Of the balance, about half are soft courts and half are grass courts

ETIQUETTE

Spectator Conduct

Whether you are a casual spectator watching an informal match or a member of a large crowd watching a championship tournament, you should be aware of some "unwritten rules." Player concentration is essential to a top performance, and anything that detracts from this concentration could affect the outcome of an entire match. The general rule is to govern your actions the way you would want others to act if you were playing. Some specific rules are:

1. Remain seated in the areas provided for spectators. Never sit on any benches or seats within the fenced area unless you have a specific function.
2. Keep quiet. Nothing is more disturbing than unnecessary conversation.
3. Applaud good play after the point is completed.
4. If you are interested in the score, keep it yourself. Do not continually bother the players by asking the score.
5. If you disagree with a decision, keep your opinion to yourself.
6. Referee a match only if acting in that official capacity. (If you are asked to serve as an umpire or linesman, you should do so willingly.)
7. If you are heading for another court, walk inconspicuously behind the fence of the court at the conclusion of the point.

Player Conduct

Good sportmanship is the key to tennis etiquette. Treat others as you desire to be treated.

The following are some specific rules that will make tennis more enjoyable for you and for those around you:

1. Know your opponent. Before you play, greet your opponent and introduce yourself.
2. Spin your racket to decide the choice of serve and side before you walk onto the court.
3. Check the net height at the center of the court. The net is 36 inches high. If you have a standard sized racket, stand your racket on the ground by the handle (27 inches) and place the edge of the racket head of your opponent (9 inches) on the top of your racket head.
4. After a brief warm-up (10-minute maximum), ask your opponent if he wishes to practice any serves. All practice serves should be taken by both players before any points are played. Never take the "first one in."

Check the net height

5. Begin a point as a server only if you have two balls in your hand.
6. Wait until your opponent is ready before serving.
7. Failure to observe the footfault rule is considered a breach of tennis etiquette.
8. Keep score accurately and, as server, periodically announce the score.
9. Return only balls that are good, especially on the serve.
10. Call the balls on your side of the net (say "out" if the ball is out), and trust your opponent to do the same. Call faults and lets loud and clear. If the ball is in, or if you are unsure, you must play the ball as good and say nothing.
11. Talk only when pertinent to the match; and then only when the ball is not in play. However, recognize a good play by your partner or opponent.
12. Control your feelings and temper.
13. Collect all balls on your side of the net after each point and return them directly to the server. Don't lean on the net to retrieve a ball — the net cables break easily. When the match is completed, leave no balls or debris on the court.
14. Retrieve balls from an adjacent court by waiting until the point is over and then politely by saying "Thank you" or "Ball, please."
15. Return balls from an adjacent court by waiting until the play in progress has been completed, and then by tossing or rolling them to the nearest player.
16. Call a "let" when there is reasonable interference during play (such as another ball entering your court).
17. Make no excuses. At the conclusion of play, shake hands with your opponent, and thank him for the match. Congratulate him if he won.
18. If others are waiting, don't monopolize the courts. Either play doubles or rotate at the conclusion of each set.
19. Always dress properly — neatly and wearing a shirt.

Tournament Conduct

1. Report to the tournament desk at least 15 minutes ahead of scheduled time. If you cannot, let the tournament desk know ahead that you may be late or must default.
2. The winner returns all balls to the tournament desk, reports the score, and ascertains his next playing time.
3. Offer to help the tournament committee (call lines, prepare courts, transportation, etc.)
4. Thank the tournament director at the end of the tourney. If room and board were provided, adequately thank those responsible.

RULES OF TENNIS

Server and Receiver

The players stand on opposite sides of the net. The player who first delivers the ball is called the server, and the other the receiver.

Spin the racket to decide who chooses first "M" or "W"

Choice of Service or Side

The choice of sides and the right to be server or receiver in the first game is decided by toss. Generally one player spins his racket and the other player calls one of the options presented by the markings on the racket ("upside-down" or "right-side-up," "M" or "W," "number" or "no number," and so on). The player winning the toss may choose, or require the opponent to choose:

1. The right to be server or receiver, in which case the other player chooses the side; or
2. The side, in which case the other player chooses the right to be server or receiver.

Players change sides after the games played in each set total an odd number — after the first game and every two games thereafter. A maximum of 1 minute is allowed for players to change sides.

Faults

The serve is a fault:

1. If the server fails to hit the ball into the proper court.
2. If the server misses the ball in attempting to strike it. (It may be tossed several times without penalty.)
3. If the ball served touches a permanent fixture (other than the net) or the server's partner before it hits the ground.
4. If a foot fault is committed.

A foot fault is called:

1. If the server changes his position by walking or running before he hits the ball. (A server may jump at the serve, and one or both feet may be over the baseline, provided he does not touch the court or line before contacting the ball.)
2. If the server touches the baseline or the court area within the baseline before he hits the ball.
3. If the server serves from outside the area between the sideline and the center mark.

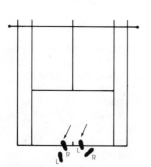

Foot faults

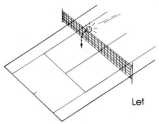

Let

Lets

A let is a served ball that touches the net, strap, or band and is otherwise good. When a let occurs on a service, the serve is replayed. When a let occurs during a play other than on a serve, the play continues uninterrupted.

A let may be called when play is interrupted or if the serve is delivered before the receiver is ready, provided the receiver has made no attempt to return the ball. In this case the point is replayed.

When Receiver Becomes Server

At the conclusion of a game, the server becomes the receiver and the receiver becomes the server.

When a Player Loses the Point

A player loses the point if:

1. He serves a double fault.
2. He fails to return the ball before it bounces twice (it may be hit before it bounces, except on the return of serve, or after it bounces once only), or if he does not return it into his opponent's court.
3. He returns the ball so that it hits the ground, a permanent fixture (fence, umpire's stand), or other object outside any of the lines that bound his opponent's court.
4. He volleys the ball and fails to make a good return even when standing outside the court.
5. He touches the ball in play with his racket more than once when making a stroke (a "double hit"), or "carries" the ball. (In doubles, the ball may be returned by only one partner.)
6. He or his racket or anything he wears or carries touches the net or the ground within the opponent's court.
7. He volleys the ball before it has passed the net.
8. The ball in play touches him or anything he wears or carries except his racket.
9. He throws his racket at and hits the ball.
10. He deliberately commits any act that hinders his opponent in making a stroke.

Good Return

It is a good return if:

1. The ball lands on the line.
2. The ball touches the net, provided it passes over it and lands in the proper court.
3. The player reaches over the net to hit a ball that has blown or rebounded back to the other side of its own accord, provided the player does not touch the net with his racket, body, or clothing.
4. The player's racket passes over the net after the ball has been returned, provided the net is not touched.
5. The player returns a ball that has hit a ball lying in the court. (A player may request a ball lying in his opponent's court to be removed, but not while the ball is in play.)
6. The ball is returned outside the post, provided it lands in the proper court.

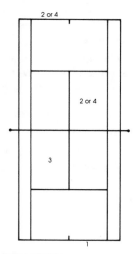

Order of serve

Order of Service in Doubles

The order of serving is decided at the beginning of each set. The pair who serve in the first game of each set decide which partner shall do so. The other partner serves the third game. The opposing pair decide who shall serve the second game of the set. The partner then serves the fourth game. This order is followed throughout the set so that each player will serve every fourth game.

If a player serves out of turn, the correct player must serve as soon as the mistake is discovered. All points earned are counted. If a complete game is played with the wrong player serving, the order of serve remains as altered.

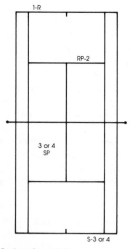

Order of receiving

Order of Receiving in Doubles

The order for receiving is determined at the beginning of each set. The receiving pair decide who is to receive the first point, and that player continues to receive the serves directed to that particular service court throughout the set. (In other words, he receives every other point in every other game.) The other partner does the same to the serves directed to the other service court.

If a player receives out of turn, he remains in that position until the game in which it is discovered is completed. The partners then resume their original positions.

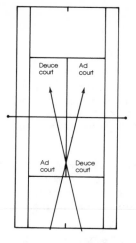

15-0	Love
30-15	15-15
40-0	30-0
40-30	30-30
	40-15
Advantage	Deuce

SCORING

The Scoring of a Game

Traditionally, points are called as follows, with the server's score always called first:

> 0 points – love
> 1st point – 15
> 2nd point – 30
> 3rd point – 40
> 4th point – game

The chart in the margin illustrates possible scoring combinations. "Deuce" means that each side has won three points. One side must now win two consecutive points to win the game. The first point after deuce is called "advantage." If the server wins it, the score is called "advantage (ad) in." If the receiver wins the first point after deuce, the score is called "advantage (ad) out."

Server has won:	Receiver has won:	Score is:
1 point	0 point	15-love
2	0	30-love
3	0	40-love
4	0	game
3	1	40-15
3	2	40-30
1	1	15-all
2	2	30-all
3	3	deuce
4	3	ad in
3	4	ad out
5	3	game (server)

No Ad Scoring

A new "sudden death" method is now used in much college play and in world team tennis. Points are scored 1, 2, 3, 4, and the first player or team to score 4 points wins the game. There is no deuce, for example. In singles or doubles if the score reaches 3–3 the receiver chooses the court from which to receive. In mixed doubles if a woman serves the 7th point, the woman on the other team receives; if a man serves, the other man receives.

The Scoring of a Set

Conventionally, the side first winning six games wins the set, provided it is ahead by at least two games. (If the score is 5–5 [5–all], play continues until someone gets two games ahead — 7–5, 8–6, etc.) An average set takes about 30 minutes to complete.

Tie Break Scoring   To help eliminate extended sets (20 –18, etc.) the USTA has authorized a best of 9 point tie break system that can be used when the score reaches 6–6 in any set. (A best of 12 point system may also be used.) The new system is played as follows:

In singles, Player A, due to serve the next regular game, serves two points, the first to the deuce court and the second to the ad court. Then Player B does the same. Sides are changed after four points and the service sequence is repeated. If neither side has won five points, Player B serves point 9. The receiver may elect to receive from either the right or left court. The set ends at 7–6. The players stay on the same side, and Player B serves the first game of the next set.

In doubles (Teams A-B vs. C-D), A and C serve the first 4 points and B and D the next 4. Player D serves the 9th point if needed. Players serve from the same sides as in the regular games.

The Scoring of a Match

A match is completed when one person or side wins two of three sets. In top men's tournaments a match usually consists of three of five sets, however. A 10-minute break is mandatory if requested by either player between the third and fourth sets, and is mandatory between the second and third sets for all youth events (16 years of age and under) although optional for boys of 16.

COMMON TENNIS INJURIES AND
HOW TO AVOID THEM

Most injuries in tennis are either muscle pulls or joint injuries. Joint injuries may be further subdivided into lower body (ankles and knees) and upper body (elbows and shoulders). Tennis is an extremely strenuous game. Often we demand more of our body than it is prepared to take. We tend to get careless about staying in condition and especially about proper warm-up. This is of special importance to those who have not played tennis for a number of years, on cold days, and the day after a strenuous match when some residual stiffness is probable.

The frequency of muscle pulls can be minimized by stretching before play begins. Some people are naturally more susceptible to muscle pulls than others. But everyone should take care to slowly stretch out the muscle groups which commonly cause problems. These are the hamstring muscles in the back of the leg, the groin muscles, and the back and stomach muscles. For muscle treatment stay warm after your match or in between matches. Don't expect too much too soon if you have a pulled muscle. Groin muscles are especially slow to heal. You must be patient.

Knee and ankle injuries are usually sprains resulting from twisting. For weak ankles it may be necessary to wear high top shoes or even tape the ankle before play to give it extra support. For weak knees, an elastic wrapping may serve as sufficient added support.

Of the joints in the upper body, the shoulders are a common problem area. Insufficient warm-up, especially on overheads and serves, can cause fiber tearing in the shoulder and internal hemorrhaging. This can lead to severe problems later on, such as calcium deposits which may require surgical removal. Take extra care to hit many easy practice serves and overheads. Swing even without the ball to simulate above-the-shoulder motions and to properly warm up this joint. You would not start your cold car and immediately drive it at 80 miles per hour: you'd let the engine idle a few minutes to warm it up and to get the oil circulating. Treat your shoulder the same way.

The elbow joint is a particular curse for tennis players. "Tennis elbow" has become increasingly common as more and more people in middle age take up the game seriously. This tendonitis, or inflammation of the tendon, can be largely eliminated with gradual and proper warm-up for all shots. Incorrect hitting of the ball can be a cause for this injury.

Players especially susceptible to tennis elbow are those who hyperextend their arm on their backhand or who use excessive wrist roll and jerkiness on their forehand. Proper hitting can partly be defined as "letting the racket do the work for you." In other words, if the swing is efficient, the momentum of the racket head will impart speed to the ball, rather than the player having to "body" or force the shot.

For the elbow (or shoulder) be very careful even at the slightest sign of strain. If a pain or heaviness persists, you might try a racket lighter in the head with a looser string job, or even softer balls, to minimize the shock of the racket meeting the ball. Perhaps you should even try "choking up" on the racket handle a little. After play, apply an icepack to the inflamed area immediately.

Don't try to be a hero. If any injury persists, see your doctor for professional diagnosis and advice. If you take good care of your body, as you would any piece of valuable machinery, you will be able to enjoy a beautiful game for a lifetime.

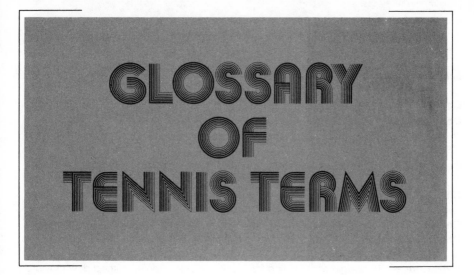

GLOSSARY OF TENNIS TERMS

Ace. A ball that is served so well that the opponent fails to touch it with his racket.

Ad. Short for advantage. It is the first point scored after deuce. If the serving side scores, it is "ad in"; if the receiving side, it is "ad out."

Ad court. The left service court, so called because an "ad" score is served there.

All. An even score: 30-all, 3-all, etc.

Alley. The area on either side of the singles court which enlarges the width of the court for doubles. Each alley is 4½ feet wide.

American twist. A serve which causes the ball to bounce high and in the opposite direction from which it was originally traveling.

Angle shot. A ball hit to an extreme angle across the court.

Approach. A shot behind which a player comes to the net.

Attack drive. An aggressive approach shot.

Australian doubles. Doubles in which the point begins with the server and his partner on the same side of the court.

Backcourt. The area between the service line and the baseline.

Backhand. The stroke used to return balls hit to the left of a right-handed player.

Backhand court. The left side of the court (for a right-handed player).

Backspin. Spin from bottom to top, applied by hitting down and through the ball. Also called underspin. **See also** Slice, Chop.

Backswing. The initial part of any swing. The act of bringing the racket back to prepare for the forward swing.

Ball boy. A person who retrieves balls for tennis players during competition.

Baseline. The end boundary line of a tennis court, located 39 feet from the net.

Bevel. The tilt or slant of the racket face.

Break service. To win a game in which the opponent serves.

Bye. The state, in competition, in which a player is not required to play in a particular round.

Cannonball. A hard, flat serve.

Center mark. The short line that bisects the center of the baseline.

Center service line. The line that is perpendicular to the net and divides the two service courts.

Center strap. A strap in the center of the net, anchored to the ground to hold the net secure.

Chip. A modified slice, used primarily in doubles to return a serve. A chip requires a short swing, which allows the receiver to move in close to return.

Choke. To grip the racket up toward the head.

Chop. A backspin shot in which the racket moves down through the ball at greater than a 45 degree angle.

Closed face. The angle of the hitting face of the racket when it is turned down toward the court.

Consolation. A tournament in which first-round losers continue to play in a losers' tournament.

Cross-court shot. A shot in which the ball travels diagonally across the net, from one corner to the other.

Deep shot. A shot that bounces near the baseline (near the service line on a serve).

Default. Failure to complete a scheduled match in a tournament; a defaulting player forfeits his position.

Deuce. A score of 40-40 (the score is tied and each side has at least three points).

Deuce court. Right court, so called because on a deuce score the ball is served there.

Dink. A ball hit so that it floats back with extreme softness.

Double elimination. A tournament in which a player or team must lose twice before he is eliminated.

Double fault. The failure of both service attempts to be good. It costs a point.

Doubles. A match with four players, two on each team.

Draw. The means of establishing who plays whom in a tournament.

Drive. An offensive ball hit with force.

Drop shot. A softly hit shot that barely travels over the net.

Drop volley. A drop shot that is hit from a volley position.

Earned point. A point won by skillful playing rather than by a player's mistake.

Elimination. A tournament in which one is eliminated when defeated.

Error. A point that ends by an obvious mistake rather than by skillful playing.

Face. The hitting surface of the racket.

Fast court. A smooth surfaced court, which allows the ball to bounce quickly and low.

Fault. An improper hit, generally thought of as a serve error.

Fifteen. The first point won by a player.

Flat shot. A shot that travels in a straight line with little arc and little spin.

Floater. A ball that moves slowly across the net in a high trajectory.

Foot fault. A fault caused by the server stepping on or over the baseline before hitting the ball in service.

Force. A ball hit with exceptional power. A play in which, because of the speed and placement of the shot, the opponent is pulled out of position.

Forecourt. The area between the net and the service line.

Forehand. The stroke used to return balls hit to the right of a right-handed player.

Forehand court. The right side of the court for a right-handed player.

Forty. A player's score when he has won three points.

Frame. The part of the racket that holds the strings.

Game. That part of a set that is completed when one player or side wins four points, or wins two consecutive points after deuce.

Grip. The method of holding the racket handle. The term given the leather covering on the handle.

Ground strokes. Strokes made after the ball has bounced, either forehand or backhand.

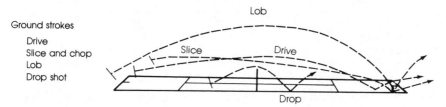

Ground strokes

    Drive
    Slice and chop
    Lob
    Drop shot

Gut. Racket strings made from animal intestines.

Half volley. Hitting the ball immediately after it bounces from the court.

Handle. The part of the racket that is gripped in the hand.

Head. The part of the racket used to hit the ball; includes the frame and the strings.

Hold serve. To serve and to win that game.

Kill. To smash the ball down hard.

Let. A point played over because of interference. A serve that hits the top of the net but is otherwise good.

Linesman. A person responsible for calling balls that land outside the court in competition.

Lob. A ball hit high enough in the air (usually clearing the net by at least 8 feet) to pass over the head of the net player.

Love. Zero; no score.

Love game. A game won without the loss of a point.

Love set. A set won without the loss of a game.

Match. Singles or doubles play that consists of two out of three sets for all women's and most men's matches, or three out of five sets for most men's championship matches.

Match point. The point which, if won, wins the match for a player.

Midcourt. The general area in the center of the playing court, midway between the net and baseline.

Mix up. To vary the type of shots attempted.

Net game. The play at the net. Also called net play.

Net play
> Drive volley
> Half volley
> and (low volley)
> Drop volley
> Overhead smash

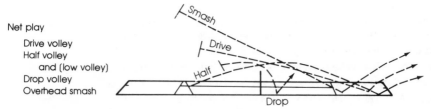

Net man. The partner in doubles who plays at the net.

No ad. Scoring system in which the first player or team to score 4 points wins the game.

No-man's-land. Midcourt, where many balls bounce at the player's feet and he is un-usually vulnerable.

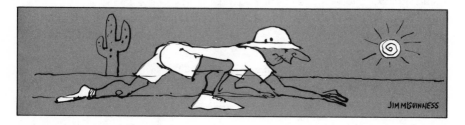

Open face. The angle of the hitting face of the racket when it is turned up, away from the court surface.

Opening. A defensive mistake that allows an opponent a good chance to score a point.

Out. A ball landing outside the playing court.

Overhead smash. **See** Smash

Overspin. **See** Topspin

Pace. Speed; usually the speed or spin of a ball which makes it skip quickly.

Passing shot. A ball hit out of reach of a net player.

Percentage tennis. "Conservative" tennis that emphasizes cutting down on unneces-sary errors and on errors at critical points.

Place. To hit the ball to the desired area.

Placement. A shot placed so accurately that an opponent cannot reach it.

Poach. A strategy whereby the net player in doubles moves over to his serving partner's side of the court to make a volley.

Press. The wooden frame that holds a wood tennis racket firmly to prevent warping.

Rally. Play in exclusion of the serve.

Retrieve. A good return of a difficult shot.

Round robin. A tournament in which every player plays every other player.

Rush. To advance to the net after hitting an approach shot.

Seed. To arrange tournament matches so that top players don't play together until the final rounds.

Serve (Service).   Method of starting the point.

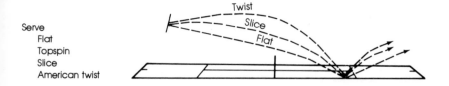

Service line.   The line that outlines the base of the service court; parallel to the baseline and 21 feet from the net.

Set.   That part of a match that is completed when one player or side wins at least six games and is ahead by at least two games, or has won the tie break.

Set point.   The point which, if won, will win the set.

Sidespin.   A shot in which the ball spins to the side and bounces to the side. The sidespin slice is one of the most common types of serve.

Singles.   A match between two players.

Slice.   A backspin shot that is hit with the racket traveling down through the ball at less than a 45 degree angle with the ground. **See also** Chip.

Slow court.   A court with a rough surface which tends to make the ball bounce rather high and slow.

Smash.   A hard overhead shot.

Spin.   Rotation of the ball caused by hitting it at an angle. **See** Topspin, Sidespin, Backspin

Straight sets.   To win a match without the loss of a set.

Tape.   The canvas band that runs across the top of the net.

Tennis elbow.   A painful condition in the elbow joint, common to tennis players and caused mostly by hyper-extension of the arm.

Thirty.   A player's score when he has won two points.

Throat.   The part of the racket between the handle and the head.

Tie break.   An official 9-point or best of 12-point sudden death scoring system when the score is 6 games all.

Topspin.   Spin of the ball from top to bottom, caused by hitting up and through the ball. It makes the ball bounce fast and long and is used on most ground strokes.

Trajectory.   The flight of the ball in relation to the top of the net.

Umpire.   The person who officiates at major matches.

Undercut.   A backspin caused by hitting down through the ball.

Underspin.   **See** Backspin, Slice, Chop.

Unseeded.   The players not favored to win and not given any special place on the draw in a tournament.

VASSS.   An unofficial ping-pong (31-point) scoring system to prevent long extended sets.

Volley.   To hit the ball before it bounces.

Wood shot.   A ball hit on the wood of the racket.